A STUDY OF HIS LIFE AND
ART WORK

BY
IRENE LANGRIDGE

PREFACE

Some years ago, I became deeply interested in William Blake, and made myself familiar with all that our public collections in London contain of his art-work. It seemed to me that this work was still so little known and appreciated by the public, that a short book might well be written to serve as a pointer to our national Blake treasures. The standard works on Blake— Gilchrist's Life, Mr. A. C. Swinburne's Critical Essay, Messrs. Ellis and Yeats' exhaustive volumes, and Mr. W. M. Rossetti's Aldine Essay—are of great literary excellence and high critical quality, and must ever remain the great authorities on the subject; but, owing to these works being either out of print, very lengthy, very expensive, or unillustrated, a want may be supplied by, and an opportunity of usefulness open to, such a book as the present one. Different in scope as it is from any other book on Blake, and modest in aim, it deals with the poet-artist as he is manifested in those works of his which are accessible to the public.

In seeking to sketch again his artistic personality, I have been guided by the conclusions of his eminent biographers and critics wherever they coincided with my own intuitive convictions. But in the study of a character and work so out of the usual, so exotic and[Pg vi] strange as those of Blake, unanimity of opinion and judgement is hardly to be hoped for, and the variety of points of view from which each new student sees him, may assist to the rounding and filling out of the portrait drawn in so masterly a manner in the first instance by Alexander Gilchrist.

My best thanks are due to Mr. A. B. Langridge for reading my proofs and for the photographs which he took expressly to illustrate this volume. Also to Mr. Frederic Shields for numerous acts of kindness and the loan of original Blake drawings, to Sir Charles Dilke, to Messrs. Chatto and Windus, to Mr. Laurence Binyon, Mr. G. K. Fortescue, and to Dr. G. C. Williamson for help given to me in various ways.

WILLIAM BLAKE

CHAPTER I
EARLY YEARS

The work of one of the greatest spirits that ever made Art his medium has yet its way to make among the general public. The world entertained the angel unawares, for three-quarters of a century have passed since the death of William Blake, and still his name and his work are but indifferently known. Yet to those that know them, the designs from his pencil, and the poems from his pen, are among the most precious things that Art has bequeathed to us.

It is my purpose in the following pages to tell over again the main outlines of his life, quite shortly and simply, for the great biography on Blake (that of Alexander Gilchrist) can be consulted by all, and contains almost every detail known about him. To this monumental work, and to Messrs. Ellis and Yeats's more recently issued and exhaustive Commentary on Blake, I owe all my facts.

A brief memoir is a necessary preface to the review I propose making of those engraved and painted books, pictures, drawings and engravings of Blake's which our National Collections possess.

William Blake was one of those unique beings who live above this actual world, in the high places of imagination. At four years old he saw his first vision, as his wife reminded him in old age, in the presence of Mr.[Pg 2] Crabb Robinson: "You know, dear, the first time you saw God was when you were four years old, and He put His head to the window and set you screaming." Quaintly, crudely, as the story is told by Mrs. Blake, it bears testimony to the fact that the visionary faculty was developed in Blake from the beginning. Imagination claimed him definitely as her child from that early day when, having rambled far afield into the country (as it was his pastime to do throughout life), he saw, in a meadow near Dulwich, a tree amongst whose branches glistening angels clustered and sang. It may be, as one of Blake's critics suggests, that Nature was herself the basis of the supernatural beauty he saw, though he was all unwitting of it. Standing beneath a tree laden with delicate pink blossom, and gazing up into the rosy gloom, Blake may well have translated this pulsating beauty into a miracle. Above among the greenery he may have seemed to catch glimpses of aspiring hands and faces among the crowding wings of flame and rose and sun-kissed gold. A little breeze would set angelic wings and garments all a-moving and a-fluttering, and a thrush's voice suddenly cleaving the silence seem an angel's song indeed, too exquisite to be endured without tears, to the quivering, spell-bound wanderer. Such *may* have been the explanation of this early vision, but Blake himself never attributed any natural cause to such spiritual manifestations. Everything was alive to him with a strange inner life: the "vegetable world," as he called it, was but the shadow of the real world of imagination, whose spiritual population was more clearly discernible to his highly-wrought consciousness, than natural phenomena themselves. Narrowly did he escape a whipping from his father, the worthy hosier, for what that matter-of-fact man could not but consider a most impudent invention on the child's part. The incident was a foreshadowing of the poet-painter's life. The[Pg 3] mysterious regions in which his spirit wandered so fearlessly, and which his poems and his drawings represented to the world, had but scanty attraction for his time. It would be truer perhaps to say that they were more often regarded with fear and repulsion. The mortal who dares to raise even the corner of the veil that so discreetly hides from our material world the many other existent conditions of consciousness, the great Beyond of Spirit Life, does so at his own risk, and with the certainty of earning his fellow men's distrust and disapproval. The outlook on that immensity has a tendency, it is true, to endanger the perfect mental equilibrium; but though the age—professing faith in a set of decent religious formulae, but in reality sceptical of all spiritual life and destiny—called Blake mad, he was recognized by a few chosen spirits as a great master and seer. The story of his life contains but few incidents, but through these incidents we see a soul travelling.

William Blake was born in 1757 at 28, Broad Street, Carnaby Market, Soho. The old house still stands, but looks very dirty and depressing, like the street, which, since Blake played in it, has suffered a dingy declension. Messrs. Ellis and Yeats, who have added some biographical details to Gilchrist's Life, state that William's father, the hosier, James Blake, was the son of an Irishman, one John O'Neil. John O'Neil married a girl from Rathmines, Dublin, called Ellen Blake, and as he soon afterwards got into debt and trouble of one sort and another, he dropped his name of O'Neil and adopted his wife's maiden name. This fact, if established beyond doubt, would seem to be of singular importance, as the presence of Irish blood in William Blake would account for several strange characteristics which are not otherwise understandable. The Kelts are always particularly sensitive and open to spiritual experience. Imagination,[Pg 4] second sight, and acute psychic consciousness, seem to be the peculiar attributes of the race; and these gifts are seldom to be found in a pure Anglo-Saxon. There were four other children, James, of whom we shall hear again, Robert, our artist's beloved younger brother, John, a ne'er-do-weel, and a girl of whom not much is known.

Very early William developed a taste for art, and his father, with more sense than usually characterizes the parents of great men, allowed him to follow his bent, and sent him, from the age of ten to fourteen, to the drawing class of one Pars, in the Strand. We read of his attending picture sales and occasionally buying drawings and prints after Raphael, Michael Angelo, Albert Dürer, and other old masters at prices which would make the modern collector green with envy. But we do not hear of Blake's attending any other school either before or after leaving Pars for the purpose of furthering his general education. All the knowledge that he acquired outside Art was self-chosen and self-taught. A sound general education is the firmest basis on which to build a tower of observation from which the world and life may be surveyed with judgement. Blake's beautiful and fantastic house of thought, however, was erected on no such foundation. Perhaps instinct guided his choice of mental food: certain it is that the peculiar education he gave himself enabled him to preserve his own personality in all its vital energy. Pars appears to have been the Squarcione of that generation. He had been sent to Greece by the Dilettante Society to study ruined temples and broken statues. On his return to England he set up a school in the Strand to teach drawing from plaster casts after the antique.

When he was fourteen, with a view to getting a trade by which he could earn his daily bread, Blake's father determined to apprentice him to an engraver. He took him first to Rylands, an eminent engraver with a Court[Pg 5] appointment, but the boy said after the interview, "Father, I do not like that man's face. He looks as if he would live to be hanged." Strange forecast this proved to be, for in 1783 Rylands was indeed hanged for forgery. Blake was finally apprenticed to Basire, a sound craftsman, but of a somewhat hard and dry manner. Basire's style as an engraver set its stamp on Blake, there is no doubt. It would have hampered most men severely, rendering their work formal and immobile, but Blake turned it to a strange account, and it became expressive in his hands. When in his later years he found that he had outgrown it, he modified it to suit his new requirements, but it had been a laborious and useful servant, if not a gracious one. During his apprenticeship Basire set him to draw all the mediaeval tombs and monuments in Westminster Abbey and other churches for a certain publication to be brought out by the firm. In doing this Blake imbibed large draughts of the intense and fervent Gothic spirit. Its deep innerness, its passionate aspiration, its whimsicality, and its quaint decorative exuberance, expressed alike in angels and gargoyles, found and touched a vibrating chord in his heart. Gothic art entered into him and became part of him. Its influence was strong, though it took a characteristically Blakeian expression always, and those long mornings spent among the slanting sunbeams and the whispering silence of the chapels around the King Confessor's tomb, were among the truly eventful incidents of his life.

In many of his designs a Gothic church with spires and buttresses like Westminster,—often a mere symbol sufficient to recall it, occasionally carefully and elaborately drawn in—stands as an embodiment of Blake's idea of worship.

Strange thoughts must have come to him among those forests of slender pillars and arches! Some hint[Pg 6] of them is conveyed by an engraving he did during the period of drawing in the Abbey. It is after a drawing (probably one bought by him cheap at a sale room) by Michael Angelo, and has the imaginative inscription written on it by Blake, "Joseph of Arimathea among the Rocks of Albion. This is one of the Gothic artists who built the cathedrals in what we call the dark ages, wandering about in sheepskin and goatskin, of whom the world was not worthy." Joseph of Arimathea, it will be remembered, is supposed to have come to Glastonbury in 63 A.D. and built the first Christian Church.

He did not always work in the Abbey in quiet. There is a story told by Messrs. Ellis and Yeats, of how he was plagued by the Westminster boys till he laid his grievance before the Dean, who thereupon deprived the boys of the right to wander about the Abbey at their pleasure, a right denied to them to this day.

At twenty, Blake's apprenticeship to Basire being ended, he attended the Academy schools and drew from the antique under Keeper Moser, picking out for his chief delight and most ardent study the drawings of Michael Angelo and Raphael—a very barbaric choice it was considered, according to the decadent taste of the period. Moser recommended him to give up poring over "those old hard, stiff, dry, unfinished works of art," and to turn his attention to Le Brun and Rubens, some of whose drawings he fetched out for Blake's inspection. Blake, however, who was never able to conceal his thoughts, nor to express them in anything but forcible terms, burst out, "These things that you call finished, are not even begun; how then can they be finished?" and comments on the incident, which he relates in his MS. notes on "Reynolds' Discourses," made in his old age, "that the man who does not know the beginning, cannot know the end of art." By this[Pg 7] he meant, that to be preoccupied as were Rubens and Le Brun, with the merely faithful representation of the beauty of the body, to dwell as an end in itself on the wonder of white shoulders, tapering fingers, and too luscious flesh, to linger in the folds and intricacies of silk and velvet robes, and to spend strength and power on these things, was mere foolishness and blundering.

Physical beauty, splendour of colour, only thrilled and arrested him when he recognized in them the symbols of an idea, when they seemed to hint of things rarer and more excellent than any purely natural or intrinsic attribute. If he could discriminate its eternal inner message, and could make it visible to the world, then was physical beauty worthy of reproduction. But he seldom dwelt on beauty for its own sake, but only when it was spiritually significant; so it is easy to see why he was inaccessible to the influence of such artists as Rubens and Le Brun.

At the Academy Schools he had the opportunity of drawing from the living model, and profited by it to a certain limited extent. But he always had an aversion to it, declaring that to his whimsical nature it "smelt of mortality." However he might and did justify his negligence of this important branch of technique, his art was necessarily weakened by it. Technique is the language of art, and is only to be obtained by frequent and laboriously faithful reference to nature. It is true that Blake's strong power of generalizing, along with his marvellous gift of recalling at desire things discriminated by him, made the achievement of technique through methods of life study a less urgent necessity to him than to other men who had no such retentive artistic memories. Essential lines Blake never failed to give, but by intention rather than from any inability he seldom gives more than these essential lines in the figures he drew and painted.

[Pg 8]After all it is possible that his power of delineating swift movement, and the great range of emotions that correspond to that, might have been injured or lost by too close an application to the artificially posed human figure. We have seen much life lost in the too close study of life, as in the otherwise exquisite work of Lord Leighton.

Blake believed that to draw from the typical forms seen by him in vision was his true purpose and aim, and the study of individual human forms filled his eye with confusion, for, as he was for ever asserting, Nature seemed to him but a faint and garbled version of the grand originals seen in imagination, that is, in truth.

While Blake was educating himself in art, he had to earn his livelihood by engraver's work, and between 1779 and 1782 one or two booksellers employed him to engrave designs after various artists. Among these artists was Stothard, to whom, in 1782, Blake was introduced. Stothard brought Flaxman and Blake together, and the three became warm friends. It was only after many years, and then through the machinations of an evil man (the publisher Cromek), that Blake became estranged from Stothard, and partially also from Flaxman.

3

In 1780 Blake exhibited his first picture in the Academy, "The Death of Earl Godwin." It was only the twelfth exhibition of the institution, and the first to be held at Somerset House. How curiously do its four hundred and eighty-seven exhibits (including wax work and a design for a fan) contrast with our mammoth Academies of to-day! Sir Joshua Reynolds, Mary Moser, Gainsborough, Angelica Kauffman, Cosway and Fuseli, were all contributors in the year of grace 1780. Blake was in sympathy with none of them save Fuseli, who, although a man greatly overrated in his day, had a real sense of the potency of the invisible world, mainly,[Pg 9] however, of that portion of it concerned with arch-fiends, witches, demons, and baleful omens.

In 1782 Blake married Catherine Bouchier, and set up housekeeping in Green Street. It appears that he had been much in love with a girl called Pollie Wood, who had jilted him. Going to stay at Richmond in a state of deep depression, he made the acquaintance of Catherine Bouchier. Messrs. Ellis and Yeats have added this detail to the first biographer's story. When she first entered the room where he sat, she was overcome by such intense emotion that she had to withdraw for awhile. She afterwards admitted that at that moment she became suddenly aware that she was in the presence of her future husband.

Small wonder that Blake felt an irresistible affinity for this charming dark-eyed girl whose fervent susceptible spirit responded so mysteriously to his own. No marriage was ever more happy. Catherine was of humble origin, and practically no education, for at the time of her marriage she was unable to read or write, but nevertheless she possessed the rare and delicate qualities necessary for the mate of a man like Blake. She early realized that the man she had married was no ordinary one, and to be of service to her dear "Mr. Blake" (as she always called him with quaint reverence), to enter into his thoughts, to smooth the path of his material life, and to conform her young and unlessoned girlhood to his difficult standard of plain living and high thinking, became her one absorbing object.

There were a few rough passages in the early days of married life, which Gilchrist indicates, but they soon disappeared. It was merely the friction and heat given off, before the two strong natures were fused into a perfect union. Catherine's nature appears to have been a compound of ardent worship and pregnant sympathy.[Pg 10] Never did a woman so forget herself in reverencing, nigh worshipping, the man she had chosen to marry.

During an unusually long, and in many respects a peculiarly isolated life, these two lived together, the one master mind and purpose informing both.

No words could do full justice to the beautiful life of Catherine Blake. It is true that no ordinary man could have drawn such harmony from the vivacious, impulsive, passionate nature of the girl. All the generous love that her nature possessed she lavished on Blake, and her complete absorption in him seems to have satisfied the maternal cravings which were to have no other satisfaction, for William and Catherine had no children. The work of caring for the few rooms which were all that Blake's means allowed, and his ambition desired, for the housing of their bodies, this Catherine did with the thoroughness of the true aesthete. She cooked, sewed, swept, dusted, and washed, and yet found time to learn from her husband how to read and write, the use of the graver, and even to colour with neat and precise hand some of the prints he made. Added to this she was soon able to read with intelligence the books he praised, and listened wondering to the songs he made, finding them of a heavenly significance and beauty; and when his tense nerves and superabundant physical energy drove Blake forth to stretch his limbs and cool his brain in long country walks of thirty, and occasionally forty miles at a stretch, Catherine went with him, and cheerfully tramped along beside him, silent or responsive as he set the mood.

Again, when in the night time visions appeared to his teeming ever-inventive brain, and he must needs get up and write or draw while the divine "mania" was upon him, then Catherine arose softly and sat beside that wondrous husband in her white nightgown, her whole consciousness hanging upon his least movement[Pg 11] or utterance, and her whole being thrilling sympathetically to those invisible presences which moved his spirit. Like Mary, "she kept all these things in her heart and pondered them."

Speaking of his wife, one cannot but recall that in Blake's mysterious and unorthodox creed the doctrine of free love was a very favourite one, on which in his poetry he was never tired of insisting. Yet he seems to have desired freedom, only, as Mr. Swinburne finely shows, "for the soul's sake." If love is bound, he argued, what merit is there in faithfulness? Love, to be what love in perfect development should be,—to be what Love in its very essence predicates,—must be free. Such a creed, proclaimed by the lips of the most austere of men in matters sensual, seems to shadow forth one dimly apprehended aspect of a truth, which may be realized perhaps, in a future and more perfect state of society.

"In a myrtle shade," and "William Bond," are two among the poems in Blake's MS. book, which have their origin in thoughts about free love.

4

The year after his marriage, 1782-83, Blake had to turn to engraving in real earnest to pay for the necessities of the modest *ménage* in Green Street. We find him engaged mainly in engraving plates after Stothard's refined and graceful designs. In after years, when he was estranged from Stothard, Blake used to say that many of these same designs contained ideas stolen from himself. There can be small doubt that Stothard did owe something to Blake's influence. Fuseli frankly declared that "Blake is damned good to steal from," and accordingly adopted his ideas, and in one instance, at least, a complete design.

A kind and appreciative couple, the Rev. Henry and Mrs. Mathew, received Blake in their drawing-room about this time, and gave him an honoured place[Pg 12]among their guests. It was they who paid in part for the production of his "Poetical Sketches," and Flaxman, who had always a strong admiration of Blake's poetical genius, helped,—an act of beautiful generosity in a young artist with his own way to make.

The "Poetical Sketches" are among the tenderest lyric notes uttered by Blake, and their bird-like spontaneity and lilt recall, says Dante Gabriel Rossetti, "the best period of English song-writing, whose rarest treasures lie scattered among the plays of our Elizabethan dramatists." These wild wood-notes gushing unselfconscious from a heart glad with youth and fair visions are in strange contrast to the artificial, trifling, and unsatisfying poetry of the age. Blake himself writes in the "Poem to the Muses":

How have you left the ancient love
That bards of old enjoy'd in you!
The languid strings do scarcely move,
The sound is forced, the notes are few.

What can be said of that perfect lyric, written when Blake was but fourteen, "My silks and fine array," and that other which I shall surely be forgiven for quoting as it stands:

How sweet I roamed from field to field
And tasted all the summer's pride,
Till I the Prince of Love beheld
Who in the sunny beams did glide.

He show'd me lilies for my hair,
And blushing roses for my brow;
He led me through his gardens fair
Where all his golden pleasures grow.

With sweet Maydews my wings are wet,
And Phoebus fired my vocal rage;
He caught me in his silken net,
And shut me in his golden cage.
[Pg 13]
He loves to sit and hear me sing,
Then, laughing, sports and plays with me;
Then stretches out my golden wing,
And mocks my loss of liberty.

To a poetically sensitive mind, verses like these remain like a beautiful echo in the memory, having a musical charm apart from the sense of the words. Although in this little book it is my purpose to dwell mainly on Blake's manifestation of himself as a designer and painter, I cannot avoid lingering sometimes on his poetical expression. For the creative impulse that clothed its thought in a garment of words is the same as that which is embodied in plastic forms and symbolic colouring. Blake's invention had two outlets, but was itself one stream of energy only.

The lines to the Evening Star are incomparably sweet and haunting:

Thou fair-hair'd angel of the evening,
Now, whilst the sun rests on the mountains, light
Thy brilliant torch of love; thy radiant crown
Put on, and smile upon our evening bed!
Smile on our loves, and whilst thou drawest round
The curtains of the sky, scatter thy dew
On every flower that closes its sweet eyes
In timely sleep. Let thy west wind sleep on
The lake; speak silence with thy glimmering eyes,
And wash the dusk with silver. Soon, full soon,

5

Dost	thou	withdraw;	then	the	wolf	rages	wide,
And	then	the	lion	glares	through	the	dim	forest,
The	fleeces	of	our	flocks	are	covered	with

Thy sacred dew; protect them with thine influence.

The lingering subtle and most musical sweetness of such lines as those quoted above, "Let thy west wind sleep on the lake; speak silence with thy glimmering eyes, and wash the dusk with silver," can be surpassed by none of the great masters of melody. So unaccustomed were the ears of the time to such perfectly[Pg 14] natural bursts of song, that the Rev. Henry Mathew considered it necessary to apologize to the refined and fastidious for calling attention to them, "hoping their poetic originality merits some respite from oblivion." Blake might well seem strange to these *borné* people, for he was no other than the herald and forerunner of the poetic renaissance of the beginning of the nineteenth century.

In the Mathew's drawing-room, surrounded by a wondering group of dilettanti, above whom he towered head and shoulders intellectually, he was encouraged to sing his "Songs of Innocence," which he had already written, though not produced, to his own music. Blake had then a mode of musical expression as well as an artistic and a literary one, though no record of it has been preserved. With these three keys he unlocked the doors of materialism outwards, on to the vistas of God-thrilled Eternity.

In 1784 Blake exhibited two drawings in the Royal Academy, "War, unchained by an Angel—Fire, Pestilence and Famine following," and "A Breach in the City—the Morning after a Battle." It is obvious from these that his style was already formed in all its strength and almost terrifying individuality.

During this year Blake's father died, and William and Catherine returned to Broad Street and took up their abode next to the paternal dwelling now occupied by the elder brother James. James, though a Swedenborgian and accounting himself a godly person, was also a busy seeker after this world's good things, and seems to have had little in common with William, though for some years friendly relations were maintained between them. Blake set up a shop as printseller and engraver in Broad Street in company with a man named Parker, whose acquaintance he had made in the old Basire days, but it was a short-lived affair, and soon came to an end.

[Pg 15]It was in this year that William's younger brother Robert became his pupil. Nothing much can be discovered about the personality of Robert, but from Blake's own writings and designs we are able to see how close a tie of affection existed between these two brothers.

Robert only lived three years after becoming William's house-mate and pupil. In his final illness it was not Catherine but William who nursed him day and night untiringly, with passionate love and care; and when at last the end came, Blake saw his brother's soul fare forth, clapping its hands for joy, from the mortal tenement—a vision to bear fruit afterwards in his designs for Blair's "Grave." Then he was beset with sheer physical exhaustion, and going to bed, slept for three days and three nights. Many years after we find him going back into this period of personal sorrow, to extract therefrom comfort for Hayley, who had lost his son.

"I know," he writes to him, "that our deceased friends are more really with us than when they were apparent to our mortal part. Thirteen years ago I lost a brother, and with his spirit I converse daily and hourly in the spirit, and see him in remembrance in the regions of my imagination. I hear his advice and even now write from his dictate. Forgive me for expressing to you my enthusiasm, which I wish all to partake of, since it is to me a source of immortal joy, even in this world. May you continue to be so more and more, and to be more and more persuaded that every mortal loss is an immortal gain. The ruins of time build mansions in Eternity":—from all of which it is easy to see that Robert's influence on the soul of William augmented after his death.

In 1788 Blake removed from Broad Street to No. 28, Poland Street, which lies in its immediate neighbourhood. A coolness may have sprung up between[Pg 16]James and William, for the brothers saw little of each other now.

The following characteristic story, taken from Mr. Tatham's MS., and retold by Messrs. Ellis and Yeats, helps to draw in Blake's psychological portrait.

In Poland Street Blake's windows looked over Astley's Yard,—Astley of circus fame. One day on looking out he saw a boy limping up and down, dragging a heavy block chained to his foot. It was a hobble used for horses, and Blake, with his brain on fire and pity and rage tearing at his heart, was soon down in the yard among the circus company. He gave them a passionate speech on liberty, appealed to them as true men and Britons not to punish a fellow-countryman in a manner that would degrade a slave, and finally saw the crowd yield to his eloquence, and his point was gained. The boy was loosed, and Blake returned to his own world of work and vision.

6

Some hours after, Mr. Astley, who had been out during the incident related, called on Blake, and stormed and raved at what he called his interference. At first Blake was as angry as Astley, his blood was up, and there seemed every prospect of a very violent quarrel. But suddenly, in the midst of his anger, Blake remembered that the amelioration of the boy's condition was his first object, and, quickly changing his tactics, he so worked on the higher moral nature which Astley evidently possessed, that he completely won him over to his views, and the two men parted—friends. Ever after, however, as Messrs. Ellis and Yeats point out, the chain remained with Blake as the symbol of cruel oppression and slavery, and we shall see him using it in his designs again and again as such.

In 1790 he produced the "Songs of Innocence," printed and published, as well as designed, engraved, and composed by himself. In the long and romantic[Pg 17]history of art, nothing is more strange than the story of how this little book came into being. Blake was unknown to the world and had no credit with publishers, nor had he the wherewithal to publish at his own expense the poems which he had written and called "Songs of Innocence." Yet he greatly desired to see them set forth in a book with appropriate and significant designs. But how was this to be accomplished? He pondered the matter long, till at last light and leading came. In the silence of one midnight his dead brother Robert appeared to him and instructed him as to the method—an entirely original one—which he should use. The very next day, Blake being urgent to begin his work, his wife went out early with half-a-crown (all the money they had in the world), and laid out one and tenpence on the necessary material. And in faith and gladness, relying on that mystical power in himself which took and used his hand and eye and brain almost without his will, he began to make the first of his lovely engraved and painted books. This is the alpha of a long series of engraved books which issued from his hand at intervals for some years. While in Poland Street he wrote, but did not publish till long after, the "Ghost of Abel," in 1789 the "Book of Thel," in 1790 the "Marriage of Heaven and Hell," and in 1791 a poem, the first of a projected series of seven books, called "The French Revolution."

This so-called poem owed its birth to the fact that about this period Blake became one of a literary, artistic, and political set who met at the house of Johnson the publisher. At these gatherings Mary Wollstonecraft arrayed her charms to storm the citadel of Fuseli's cynical heart, unavailingly. Among other guests were Tom Paine, author of "The Rights of Man," whom eventually Blake was the means of saving, by a timely word of warning, from arrest in England.[Pg 18] He judiciously advised his flight to France, at the right moment for his safety. Godwin and Holcroft and several revolutionary dreamers were members of this *coterie*. Blake's enthusiasm was set all aglow by a philosophy which saw in the French Revolution a great renovating process,—the fire to burn up the ignorance and superstition and class boundaries of the ancient order, the introduction of a new reign of righteousness and peace.

In effect, this new philosophy which fired the imagination of Blake had a basis of materialism and violence which would have found no answering response in his soul, had he sought to investigate it. His sympathy with the group was intellectual, and with the higher manifestations of its creed alone. It led to no political action. He had far other work to do than that of a political agitator, but all expansive doctrines which made for liberty and individuality fired the imagination and fed the intellect of Blake. Democracy was his ideal, and democratic virtues won his admiration; indeed, he dared to flaunt the *"bonnet rouge"* of liberty in London streets in this agitated period, but after the Days of Terror in '92 he tore off the white cockade and never again donned the Cap of Liberty. But if his work was not to be in the political arena, he was in his own way hastening the coming of that better and more immaterial kingdom which these young liberators only half conceived.

In 1792 died the great leader of English art, Sir Joshua Reynolds. His work, concerned as it was with the exquisite graces of this passing world, had nothing to say to Blake, who regarded it in the light of his own artistic standpoint, with positive aversion. It often happens that a man who feels it his burning mission to work out and reveal some hitherto neglected or unseen aspect of truth, does so at the cost of a one-sidedness[Pg 19] which is a necessary defect of his quality. Blake could no more appreciate Sir Joshua—at least at this stage of his being—than Sir Joshua could appreciate Blake. The veteran Reynolds once told him, when a young man, "to work with less extravagance and more simplicity, and to correct his drawing." Blake never got over that. We can imagine the suppressed heat with which he listened choking to the advice of the popular artist who was so utterly ignorant of his aims and ideals. To us, who may enter into the soul of each, it is given to realize that they, and all the company of the world's great artists, have furthered the true work of art; have all helped, and are helping, according to their gifts and in their degree, to rear the walls and set with windows and crown with battlements and towers, the palace of beauty for the soul of man to dwell in with delight and worship. That the workers have not always recognized each other is matter for regret, though it is scarcely perhaps to be wondered at, seeing that each is set on emphasizing and relieving against its background the one point which seems to him necessary and valuable.

The characteristic notes which Blake appended to Reynolds' "Discourses" many years later, express much of his dislike. Truly, it is easy to conceive of a mind offering nothing but delight and admiration to Reynolds' practice, yet excited to a grave disapproval by much of his theory, or what he states as his theory. For Reynolds actually taught that genius—such as his own, for instance—was a state to be inducted into by precept, and evolved through study, instead of being a thing of fire, a tongue of flame from on high, set on a man as a seal, from which he cannot escape. I am reminded of Rossetti here, who quite sincerely told Mr. Hall Caine, "I paint by a set of unwritten but clearly-defined rules, which I could teach to any man as systematically as[Pg 20] you could teach arithmetic." Ah! that such genius *might* thus be taught!

However, Reynolds, his practice and theory alike, were by Blake swept into a limbo of unconditional condemnation, though occasionally, in spite of the prejudice he nursed against Sir Joshua, he flashed out notes of emphatic approval, on certain utterances in the great man's "Discourses."

CHAPTER II
LIFE AT FELPHAM

In 1793 Blake removed across the river to Hercules Buildings, Lambeth, where he lived for seven years of great mental and spiritual vitality, seeing visions and dreaming dreams and embodying them in beautiful designs. He was a tireless worker, never resting, and sleeping much less than other men. These Lambeth days were days of comparative prosperity with the Blakes, whose wants were so simple and few. The little house in which they lived possessed rustic charms—a garden with a summer-house, and a vine climbing over the back of the house, whose leaves made a pleasant rustling in summer. A view of the river, too, could not have failed to add a significant charm to the place. On its shining surface might be descried ships like souls faring to the world's great market-place, to barter and to receive merchandise; while others, with white sails set, slipped quietly down the river and out to the wide mysterious sea. Blake had a few pupils, too, and at this period he made the acquaintance of Mr. Butts, who was a staunch friend and true appreciator for thirty years. During all that time he was a constant buyer of our artist's work, and bought sometimes at the rate of one drawing a week. In time Mr. Butts' spacious house in Fitzroy Square became a regular Blake Gallery. The average price he paid was £1 to 30s. a design or[Pg 22] picture. To Mr. Butts' great honour be it said that he never assumed the airs of a patron, never tried to bind or hamper Blake's genius, or to dictate or direct his choice of subjects or treatment of them. He seems to have realized that this man was "a prince in Israel," and the lordship of his ideas not to be questioned, but accepted humbly and with gratitude.

In a future chapter I hope to deal with the Blake drawings and easel pictures done for Mr. Butts, which were available to the public in the Exhibition at Messrs. Carfax's Rooms in Ryder Street, held in 1904.

Blake seems to have enjoyed a little wave of recognition at Lambeth—popularity it can hardly be called—but it was not long-lived. At one time he was even suggested as drawing-master to the Royal Family, but declined the position, not from modesty, but from devotion to his true *métier*—the preservation and expression of spiritual ideas—with which such a post would probably have interfered.

Two acts of secret and most munificent generosity are recorded by Tatham, and quoted by Messrs. Ellis and Yeats, concerning Blake while at Lambeth.

He gave £40 (he seldom after had half as much money beside him) to a friend in distress, and his deep sympathetic heart being moved by the sight of a sick young man, an artist, who daily passed their door, he and his Kate made the young man's acquaintance, and for the love of Christ and in memory of brother Robert, finally took him into their house and tended him till his death some months later.

While at Lambeth he made three large and important drawings—"Nebuchadnezzar," an enlarged edition of the bearded figure on hands and knees which occurs in "The Marriage of Heaven and Hell"; "The Lazar House" and "The Elohim creating Adam." He also[Pg 23] made designs for Young's "Night Thoughts." There were 537 designs made, and Blake only took a year to do them. A selected few were engraved. While at Lambeth he printed also his "Visions of the Daughters of Albion," "America," "Europe," "Urizen," "The Gates of Paradise," "The Book of Los," "The Song of Los," and "Ahania." The list implies steady application, and untiring intellectual and spiritual energy.

8

The introduction of our painter, in 1800, by his old friend Flaxman, to Hayley, poetaster and dilettante, marks the beginning of a new epoch in his life.

Hayley, the friend of Gibbon and, later, of Cowper (whose biography he wrote), was a characteristic product of the last quarter of the eighteenth century,—that age of complaisant preoccupation with trifles.

This poetically barren interval before the birth of the wonderful new school of poetry had, since the best days of Cowper, but one star above its horizon—or was it a will-o'-the-wisp?—the *soi-disant* poet Hayley. Complaisantly he twinkled on his admiring world, and, striking the lyre with gracious hand, sang with modest satisfaction "The Triumphs of Temper." This now forgotten work earned him the position of "greatest of living poets," and he assumed his high seat in the literary world with bustling alacrity. Above all things he aspired to culture, not at the expense of a very continuous effort or strain, it is true, but he loved to collect around him artists and men of letters to whom he could play the part of a somewhat undersized Lorenzo de' Medici. That they would respond gracefully, and take their parts becomingly in this garden-comedy, was all that he required of his court.

It will be remembered that Romney was one of his artist friends, and that the connection proved in a way economically disastrous to the painter, for Hayley was an extravagant man, though he professed simple tastes,[Pg 24] and encouraged poor Romney in his mania for building and other lavish expenditure.

His influence, such as it was, was stimulating to none of his friends, though he meant well and kindly enough. He affected the part of the country gentleman, as well as that of the high priest of culture, and delighted in patronage.

Soon after his acquaintance with Blake began, his old friend Cowper died under tragic conditions, and a week later Hayley's only child (an illegitimate son) died also. The boy was a youth of promise, and had been a pupil of Flaxman. So he had gratified as well as filled the poor father's heart. Hayley's trouble called forth a letter from Blake, which I quoted when writing on the death of Robert, and it seems to have touched, perhaps comforted, Hayley, who even in his deep affliction assumed a pose not natural or spontaneous.

Blake was recommended by Flaxman as an engraver and designer (if the latter should be required), and Hayley proposed that the Blakes should come and live at Felpham, near his own place of Eartham in Sussex, in order that his new *protégé* might engrave the illustrations to the life of Cowper which he was now about to write, under Hayley's own eye.

The idea pleased Blake, while Mrs. Blake, he wrote, "is like a flame of many colours of precious jewels, whenever she hears it named." As a matter of fact, Hayley did not live at Eartham now, as the place was an expensive one to keep up, but had built himself a wonderful turretted marine "cottage," with a library and covered court for equestrian exercise at Felpham.

In the September of 1800, Blake being then forty-three years old, the husband and wife took up their abode in a pretty little cottage by the sea at Felpham, and began a new manner of life. If Hercules Buildings, Lambeth, had afforded Blake hints and types of spiritual[Pg 25] life and light, how much larger a vista must have opened to him at Felpham. He used to wander musing along the seashore, and more than once saw the yellow sands peopled by a host of souls long since departed from this earth—Moses and the Prophets, Homer, Dante, Milton: "all," Blake said, "majestic shadows, gray but luminous, and superior to the common height of men." Many visions came to him at first. It is not wonderful that this should have been so, for there was nothing that did not teem with suggestions to his subjective mind, and when he received a new influx of spiritual light, as he seemed to have had at Felpham, then, indeed, were blossoms, stars and stones, nay, the very air he breathed, alive with a strange, sentient, crowding population, to whose spiritual utterances he listened, whose forms he strained his mental sight to realize.

In a letter to Flaxman, beginning, "Dear Sculptor of Eternity," Blake writes in the first effervescence of delight: "Felpham is a sweet place for study, because it is more spiritual than London. Heaven opens here on all sides her golden gates; her windows are not obstructed by vapours; voices of celestial inhabitants are more distinctly heard, and their forms more distinctly seen."

For a while all went very well indeed, and the first part of his sojourn at Felpham was a sort of charmed circle in his life. "Mr. Hayley acts like a prince," "Felpham is the sweetest spot on earth," "work will go on here with God-speed," "Find that I can work with greater pleasure than ever," are phrases which occur in the enthusiastic letters of the period. But gradually Hayley's constant companionship, his amiable but fatuous and gushing friendship, acted like the hated chain of slavery on Blake's electric and expansive temperament. Hayley's mind was set on little things, trivial business and futile undertakings, and his vanity and self-satisfaction about all his doings came at last to be[Pg 26] exasperating to Blake. In spite of his generosity, his lavish but undiscerning praise, and the commissions for engraving and designs with which he supplied our

9

artist, Blake little by little found himself goaded to madness by the ever-flowing stream of Hayley's conventionality and watery enthusiasms. Hayley attempted to enlarge Blake's education by reading to him Klopstock and translating as he went along—a proceeding that must have bored our fiery genius to tears. He also, with the kindest intentions in the world, obtained commissions for Blake to paint miniatures—hardly, one would think, a congenial form of art to him, but one which at the beginning appears to have interested him nevertheless.

A couplet he wrote in the Note-book at the time evidences the irritated nerves that Hayley's unspiritual contact set on edge:

Thy   friendship   oft   has   made   my   heart   to   ache.
Do be my enemy for friendship's sake.

The letters, too, to Mr. Butts give direct insight into his state of mind, and the points of sharp disagreement and intellectual misunderstanding between the two men are easily traced.

It appears that "Hayley was as much averse to a page of Blake's poetry as to a chapter in the Bible."

Blake the creator and artist was unintelligible and foreign to Hayley, who, always satisfied with his own judgement, sought to turn Blake from designing and to chain him to the hack work of engraving.

By degrees the visions that had so often and radiantly appeared to Blake on his first coming to Felpham seemed to forsake him. As he became involved in Hayley's pursuits, and sought to work out Hayley's plans for him, the visions even appeared to be angry with him. Then, indeed, it seemed that he was in danger of "bartering his birthright for a mess of pottage." He writes to Mr. Butts:

[Pg 27]"My unhappiness has arisen from a source which, if explored too narrowly, might hurt my pecuniary circumstances, as my dependence is on engraving at present, and particularly the engravings I have in hand for Mr. H., and I find on all hands great objections to my doing anything but the mere drudgery of business, and intimations that if I do not confine myself to this, I shall not live. This has always pursued me.... This from Johnson and Fuseli brought me down here, and this from Mr. H. will bring me back again. For that I cannot live without doing my duty to lay up treasures in heaven, is certain and determined, and to this I have long made up my mind.... But," he goes on to say, "if we fear to do the dictates of our angels, and tremble at the tasks set before us; if we refuse to do spiritual acts because of natural fears and natural desires, who can describe the dismal torments of such a state? I too well remember the threats I heard" (*i.e.*, in vision). "If you, who are organized by Divine Providence for spiritual commission, refuse and bury your talents in the earth, even though you should want natural bread—sorrow and desperation pursue you through life, and after death shame and confusion of face to eternity. Everyone in eternity will leave you, aghast at the man who was crowned with glory and honour by his brethren and betrayed their cause to their enemies. You will be called the base Judas who betrayed his friend."

Blake was the apostle and martyr of this devotion to the high spiritual mission of Art. He would make no compromise with the world.

In a letter to Mr. Butts dated April 25th, 1803, he writes:

"I can alone carry on my visionary studies in London unannoyed, and that I may converse with my friends in Eternity, see visions, dream dreams, and prophesy and speak parables, unobserved, and at liberty from the[Pg 28] doubts of other mortals, perhaps doubts proceeding from kindness, but doubts are always pernicious, especially when we doubt our friends. Christ is very decided on this point: 'He who is not with me is against me;' there is no medium or middle state; and if a man is the enemy of my spiritual life, while he pretends to be the friend of my corporeal, he is a real enemy; but the man may be the friend of my spiritual life while he seems the enemy of my corporeal, though not *vice versâ*."

This enemy to Blake's spiritual life is certainly Hayley.

He writes with unmistakable frankness of the Hermit of Eartham in a later letter:

"Mr. H. approves of my designs as little as he does of my poems, and I have been forced to insist on his leaving me, in both, to my own self-will; I am determined to be no longer pestered with his genteel ignorance and polite disapprobation. I know myself both Poet and Painter, and it is not his affected contempt that can move to anything but a more assiduous pursuit of both arts. Indeed, by my late firmness I have brought down his affected loftiness, and he begins to think I have some genius, as if genius and assurance were the same thing! But his imbecile attempts to depress me only deserve laughter." He goes on to say that he will relinquish all engagements to design for Hayley, "unless altogether left to my own judgement, as you, my dear friend, have always left me; for which I shall never cease to honour and respect you." And for which, we may add, posterity also has good reason to laud and acclaim Mr. Butts.

Blake was not the man to be the creature of any patron, spending his time and all his magnificent powers as the servant of another man's brain—especially when that brain was Hayley's.

If the engravings and designs done for his patron[Pg 29] had earned him thousands instead of a mere competence, such work could not have tempted him from his chosen path of spiritual art. Finally, in 1803, he threw off the yoke decisively, turned his back on patronage, and returned with his faithful Kate to the liberty and poverty of rooms in South Molton Street, London, after a three years' rural seclusion. Just before leaving Felpham Blake became involved in a very disagreeable affair with a drunken soldier named Schofield, which resulted in a trial for sedition. The soldier, who was forcibly removed by Blake from his cottage garden, where he was trespassing, trumped up in revenge a set of ridiculous charges against him, saying he had used seditious language against the king and government. In the practical difficulties that all this gave rise to, Hayley came forward to Blake's assistance, and putting all the weight of his local position and popularity on the artist's side, materially helped him before and at the time of the trial. Although he had been thrown from his horse and hurt a few days previously, he insisted on being present to give evidence in his *protégé's* favour, who was of course acquitted. Warm-hearted Blake felt a generous inrush of the old affection for his friend, and a deep sense of gratitude helped to re-establish the old cordial relations between the two men. It must not be inferred from this, however, that Blake had altered his opinion that Hayley was his spiritual enemy. That, he held, Hayley had proved himself to be. But he now recognized that it was not malignity, but deficiency of spiritual knowledge and insight that had made him act as he did. It was the law of his being, and Blake, having learned this through experience of his three years' stay at Felpham, expected no more from him than his capacity warranted, and gave him his dues, dwelling with gratitude on the fact that Hayley was at least a true "corporeal friend."

[Pg 30]The stress and strain connected with the trial had a bad effect on Blake's highly-sensitive nerves, and is painfully apparent in the writing of the time. The time at Felpham, and the period that succeeded on his return to London, have much light shed on them by the Note-book. The MS. book to which reference has been made was a sort of safety valve, which Blake kept ever at his elbow, and in which he wrote long dissertations on Art and Religion—the "Public Address," the "Vision of the Last Judgment," and many of the poems published under the title (which heads the Note-book itself) of "Ideas of Good and Evil." Along with, and interspersed with these connected and finished utterances, are splenetic epigrams, rude rather than humorous caricature couplets, little scraps of unconsidered verse written to illustrate some incident of the day, and drawings here, there, and everywhere. The MS. Note-book is a very intimate part of Blake. On its first page Messrs. Ellis and Yeats quote the inscription written by Dante Gabriel Rossetti, who possessed it till his death:

"I purchased this original MS. of Palmer, an attendant at the Antique Gallery of the British Museum, on the 30th April, 1849. Palmer knew Blake personally, and it was from the artist's wife that he had the present MS., which he sold me for 10*s*. Among the sketches are one or two profiles of Blake himself." Unfortunately it has now passed by purchase into the possession of a collector at Boston, U.S.A. I say unfortunately, because our own National Museum should have secured such a treasure, but its present owner courteously lent it for a prolonged period to Messrs. Ellis and Yeats, who have embodied the main part of it in their exhaustive and most interesting work. The Note-book was deeply studied by Gilchrist, and was one of Rossetti's dearest treasures, leaving its impress on his mind and work.

[Pg 31]The work Blake did during the Felpham period included the designs and engraving of animals to Hayley's "Ballads," some of the engravings for "The Life of Cowper," and, above all, the writing of two long prophetic books, the "Milton" and the "Jerusalem," which, however, he did not finish till he had returned to London.

[Pg 32]

CHAPTER III
THE PROCESSION OF THE PILGRIMS

Blake's course was now definitely chosen. He had turned his back on patronage and voluntarily married poverty, like St. Francis, in order that he might be free to work out his own poetic and artistic ideas without reference to popularity, patronage, or pecuniary advantage. His wants and Catherine's were simple indeed, and to pay for them, from week to week, was all he desired. South Molton Street, in which they now took up their abode, was closely shut in by streets and houses. There was no garden, no summer-house or vine with pattering green leaves against the window as at Lambeth,—no trees even to recall the natural beauties of Felpham. But

Blake seems to have been almost glad to be delivered from the agitating beauty of the natural or "vegetative world," as he called it, which was to him error and not truth—the visible shadow that darkened and hid invisible and eternal ideas. Now indeed, with nothing to distract him, he could open his eyes inward into the "World of Thought," into "Eternity," which is imagination. Gilchrist's Life enables us to realize how he could live in this imaginative world, and yet, at the same time, fulfil with great practical ability such a work, for instance, as collecting material for Hayley for the "Life of Romney," which the latter was now beginning. The letters he wrote to Hayley at the time, which are all given in the Life, are the letters of a[Pg 33] kindly business-like man, intent on giving only such information as will be useful. The good sense, the sanity, the mediocrity (I had almost said) of these letters are a pledge of Blake's ability to act and express himself as other men when he wished so to do.

Hayley was his good "corporeal friend," to whom he was grateful for "corporeal acts" of kindness, and as such he treated him.

In one of the letters alone there bursts forth a great full-throated shout of joy, as it were, because he has suddenly achieved a great advance in his art. As the passage gives valuable insight into his mind at the time, I shall take liberty to quote it:

"O glory! O delight! I have entirely reduced that spectrous Fiend to his station, whose annoyance has been the ruin of my labours for the last passed twenty years of my life. He is the enemy of conjugal love, and is the Jupiter of the Greeks, an iron-hearted tyrant, the ruiner of ancient Greece. I speak with perfect confidence and certainty of the fact which has passed upon me. Nebuchadnezzar had seven times passed over him, I have had twenty; thank God, I was not altogether a beast as he was; but I was a slave bound in a mill among beasts and devils; these beasts and these devils are now, together with myself, become children of light and liberty, and my feet and my wife's feet are free from fetters....

"Suddenly on the day after visiting the Truchsessian Gallery of Pictures, I was again enlightened with the light I enjoyed in my youth, and which has for exactly twenty years been closed from me as by a door and by window shutters. Consequently I can, with confidence, promise you ocular demonstration of my altered state on the plates I am engraving after Romney, whose spiritual aid has not a little conduced to my restoration to the light of Art. O, the distress I have undergone,[Pg 34] and my poor wife with me; incessantly labouring and incessantly spoiling what I had done well. Every one of my friends was astonished at my faults, and could not assign a reason; they knew my industry and abstinence from every pleasure for the sake of study, and yet—and yet—and yet there wanted proofs of industry in my works. I thank God with entire confidence that it shall be so no longer: he is become my servant who domineered over me, he is even as a brother who was my enemy. Dear Sir, excuse my enthusiasm, or rather madness, for I am really drunk with intellectual vision whenever I take a pencil or graver into my hand, even as I used to be in my youth, and as I have not been for twenty dark but very profitable years. I thank God that I courageously pursued my course through darkness."

All of which tense and highly-figurative language means that Blake had suddenly received enlightenment on various technical methods from the silent witness of Raphael's and Michael Angelo's and other masters' achievement. He could never learn by verbal advice, precept or criticism, but when shown great work, the artist in him dwelt on every line, absorbing and assimilating its principles. The spectrous fiend to whom he refers is, according to Messrs. Ellis and Yeats, his own "selfhood." He held that every man contained in himself a devil and an angel, the devil being the natural man, the angel the God in man. Of this idea of his more hereafter.

Blake's work, when done in the heat of his spirit, is always noble, characteristic, and *largely, often wholly, right* (I am speaking of the execution, not the ideas expressed), but when "incessant labour" was expended without the incessant reference to nature which an elaborate technique demands, it is not wonderful that "incessant spoiling" should have been the result.

Now, indeed, he seems to have seen how it was with[Pg 35] himself, and to have gained a new mastery of material through studying the manner of other men's work.

In 1804 Blake brought out his "Jerusalem; the Emanation of the Giant Albion," a poem which he told Mr. Butts was descriptive of the "spiritual acts of his three years' slumber on the banks of Ocean."

"Milton" was also produced in the same year.

In 1805 Robert Hartley Cromek, whilom engraver, but now publisher and printseller, "discovered" Blake in his self-chosen retirement, and proposed giving him employment. The story of his treacherous dealings is an evil one.

Cromek, who had learnt engraving in the studio of Bartolozzi, found it laborious and slow work, so exchanged its drudgery for the calling of a publisher, but, having good taste but no capital, he was hard pressed indeed to make both ends meet.

One day a piece of luck came in his way. He paid a visit to Blake's working and living room in South Molton Street. Many beautiful things were to come into being in that room, but none more so than the drawings for Blair's "Grave" which Blake had designed, intending to print and publish them in the usual way. Cromek found them, and seized upon them, gloating. He persuaded Blake to relinquish the idea of publishing them himself, and to surrender the undertaking to Cromek as one more fitted to push them and bring them before the notice of the public.

Blake was very poor at the time. In an insulting letter written by Cromek to Blake some two years later, he refers with contemptible want of feeling and taste to this fact. "Your best work, the illustrations to the 'Grave,'" he says, "was produced when you and Mrs. Blake were reduced so low as to be obliged to live on half a guinea a week!"

Blake sold the twelve drawings to him for £1 10s.[Pg 36] each, with the assured verbal agreement that he was himself to engrave them for the projected edition—a promise which of course entailed considerable further payment for the work of engraving later on.

Cromek in possession of the copyright conveniently forgot his promise. Impregnated as he was with the fluent and graceful style of Bartolozzi's school, Blake's manner of engraving seemed to him grim, austere and archaic. He thought that the noble drawings translated by the hand of the popular and graceful engraver, Lewis Schiavonetti, would insure the success of the designs with the public as Blake could never have done were he to have engraved them himself.

It may be that there was truth in it. Some critics hold that the illustrations to Blair's "Grave" have a suavity, a felicity superimposed by the engraver on the stern and original work of Blake which was just what was needed to render his work attractive to the public. To Blake's true lovers, however, his own graver is the rightful interpreter of his own drawings, and, whether Cromek were right or not in this critical matter of taste, he was dishonest and mean to break the engagement on the basis of which alone he had obtained the drawings.

While Blake was looking forward with "anxious delight" to the engraving of his designs, Cromek had other schemes afoot. He called often at South Molton Street, hoping to pounce on some other work of genius which he could turn into money for himself. He was arrested one day before a pencil sketch of a new and hitherto untreated subject—the Procession of Chaucer's Canterbury Pilgrims. He tried to get Blake to make a finished drawing of it, with a view of course to getting it out of the artist's hands, and then having it engraved by someone else. Negotiations on this basis failing, he gave Blake a commission (verbal again) to[Pg 37] execute the design in a finished picture and an engraving from it. On the strength of this, Blake's friends circulated a subscription paper for the engraving, and he himself set to work on the picture. Cromek, however, had not done. He was in love with the subject. Sure of Blake's conception being thoughtful and strong, but probably wishful that it might be invested with a more earthly grace and interest than he would put upon it, he went to Stothard and suggested the subject to him, suppressing all mention of Blake. Probably he assisted the suggestion by hints as to its treatment derived from what he had actually appreciated in Blake's conception. He commissioned him to paint the picture for sixty guineas, an engraving from which was to be done by Bromley, though Schiavonetti was eventually substituted for him.

When Blake learned that Cromek denied having given him a commission, and came to know that Stothard, his old friend, was to paint a picture on his stolen idea, to supersede his own, his rage and indignation knew no bounds, and he became bitterly estranged from Stothard, believing in his haste "that all men are liars," and that this man had been a party to the whole mean transaction. Gilchrist is almost sure that Stothard knew nothing of Cromek's previous deal with Blake on the subject of the Canterbury Pilgrimage.

During 1806 Blake was moved to make some designs to Shakespeare which were neither commissioned nor engraved. Judging from the one reproduced in the Life,—"Hamlet and the Ghost of his Father,"—they must have been wild and powerful indeed. He had always a profound reverence for, and joy in, Shakespeare, whose works were among his favourite books.

A strange and characteristic collection were those books which fed his fiery imagination. Could we have glanced along the row, we should have seen Shakespeare[Pg 38] cheek by jowl with Lavater and Jacob Boehmen, while Macpherson's "Ossian," Chatterton's "Rowley," and the "Visions" of Emmanuel Swedenborg helped to fill in the ranks. Milton held perhaps the most honoured place of all, while Ovid, St. Theresa's works, and De la Motte Fouqué's "Sintram" were among the heterogeneous collection. Chaucer was also cheerfully conspicuous, and, towards the close of Blake's life, Dante's "Divine Comedy" came to join the silent company in the bookshelves.

In 1806 Blake became acquainted with a good and kindly man, Dr. Malkin, Head Master of Bury Grammar School. He gave him a commission for the frontispiece of Malkin's "Memorials of his Child," and in the preface wrote an account of the childhood and youth of the designer. Ozias Humphrey, the miniature painter, and a staunch friend of Blake, bought many of his engraved books, and it was he who obtained a commission for him from the Countess of Egremont to paint a picture elaborated from the Blair drawing of the "Last Judgment." The paper called by the same name in the MS. book is descriptive of this picture, and in its *intimité* and demonstration of Blake's bed-rock foundations of thought and artistic principles, gives profound insight into his mind.

These things occupied him during 1807. During that year Stothard's cabinet picture was publicly exhibited, and drew thousands of gazers. Blake doggedly continued to work at his own "Canterbury Pilgrimage," which he wrought in a water-colour medium which he arbitrarily termed "fresco." It was finished about the end of 1808. In the autumn of that year the twelve beautiful engravings after his designs for Blair's "Grave" were produced by Cromek, with a flowery introduction by Fuseli. The list of subscribers for the book at two-and-a-half guineas a copy was so large—thanks to[Pg 39] Cromek's skilful manipulation—that the amount realized by its sale came to £1,800. Of this Blake received twenty guineas and Schiavonetti about £500. I cannot omit to mention that leave to dedicate to Queen Charlotte having previously been obtained, Blake made a vignette drawing with some grave and beautiful verses to accompany it, and sent it to Cromek as an additional plate, asking the modest price of four guineas for it.

The design and verses were returned with a long letter from Cromek, closely packed with insults and slanders, and exhibiting a meanness too contemptible for expression. At the end of the letter he thus refers to the subject of the Pilgrimage, of which one would suppose he would be too ashamed to speak: "Why did you so *furiously rage* at the success of the little picture of the Pilgrimage? Three thousand people have now *seen it and have approved of it.* Believe me, yours is 'the voice of one crying in the wilderness.'

"You say the subject is *low* and *contemptibly treated.* For his excellent mode of treating the subject the poet has been admired for the last four hundred years; the poor painter has not yet the advantage of antiquity on his side, therefore with some people an apology may be necessary for him. The conclusion of one of Squire Simpkins' letters to his mother in the 'Bath Guide' will afford one. He speaks greatly to the purpose:

	I		very		well			know
Both	my	subject	and	verse	is	exceedingly		low,
But	if	any *great*	*critic* finds	fault	with	my		letter,

He has nothing to do but to send you a better.

	"With	much	respect	for	your	talents,
"I			remain,			Sir,
"Your		real	friend	and		well-wisher,

"R. H. CROMEK."

[Pg 40]Perhaps it was that last jeering taunt which determined Blake to show *his* "Canterbury Pilgrimage" to the public, and make it the occasion of a little exhibition of his own. It was opened in May, 1809. Poor unworldly Blake, enraged and baffled, was the last man to organize an undertaking of this sort. Cromek could afford to laugh at the modest show on the first floor of James Blake's shop at the corner of Broad Street, all unadvertised and unpatronized as it was.

The exhibition comprised, besides the "Pilgrimage," sixteen "Poetical and Historical Inventions," ten "frescoes," and seven drawings—"a collection," as Gilchrist remarks, "singularly remote from ordinary sympathies or even ordinary apprehension."

Few of the general public penetrated here, but Blake's friends, his few buyers, and many contemporary artists probably went through the rooms with no little curiosity. Seymour Kirkup—the discoverer of Giotto's portrait of Dante in the Bargello,—and Henry Crabb Robinson were among the number of those who went and purchased catalogues. With the catalogue were issued subscription papers for the engraving of the "Canterbury Pilgrimage," which, in spite of Cromek and Stothard, Blake intended to execute.

Blake drew up a Descriptive Catalogue to interpret his pictures, and in it gave free rein, unfortunately, to his personal antipathy to Stothard, but he also expressed at some length, and with characteristic fire and intemperance, his views on art. Dante Gabriel Rossetti, who was intensely sympathetic with his artistic forerunner, says that the Descriptive Catalogue, and the "Address to the Public," "abound in critical passages, on painting and poetry, which must be ranked without reserve among the very best things ever said on either subject."

It may be remarked, however, with all respect and[Pg 41] honour, that neither Blake nor Rossetti were critics in any exact sense of the word. The unprejudiced and scientific character of mind which analyses, classifies, and lays bare with sharp dissecting knife the structure, bones, muscles, heart, of an artistic creation, belonged to neither of them. The analytic and synthetic qualities are seldom united in one mind. (Goethe recognized this when he wrote, "I, being an artist, prefer that the principles through which I work should be hidden from me.") Both Blake and Rossetti leaped with unerring instinct and the artistic intuition at all noble and right work, and loved it with passion, rather than appreciated it with cold reason. Blake's affinities in art, for instance, especially as he grew older, were much more catholic than it would be supposed. Although the Descriptive Catalogue would induce us to believe that works of art which he did not worship were loathed by him, this was only the case when he was doing battle for certain cherished principles, and then he would hit blindly to right and left in the heat of his partisanship. Mr. Samuel Palmer spoke of evenings spent with him in his old age looking over reproductions of the pictures of various masters, which Blake enjoyed greatly, dwelling on whatever was beautiful and true in each. The Catalogue and Address were written by him with a pen steeped in wormwood. His attacks were mainly directed against the "Venetian and Flemish demons," with their "infernal machine Chiaro Oscuro," and the "hellish brownness" with which he says they and their school and modern followers load their paintings. It is true that the English school of the day feared colour, and gave a brown tone to nearly all its pictures, but probably Blake had never seen good examples of the Venetians, whose chief glory is that they "conceived colour heroically." He enunciated his own principle in these words: "The great and golden rule of art, as[Pg 42] well as of life, is this: that the more distinct, sharp and wiry the bounding line, the more perfect the work of art; and the less keen and sharp, the greater is the evidence of weak imitation, plagiarism and bungling." His mood was exasperated, truculent, passionately prejudiced, though there is much here of artistic insight and originality. It must be admitted that a great deal is painful reading, but through all the unmeasured language one feels the labouring, overstrained, noble, human heart, tormented beyond endurance. He had been galled to this state of Titanic fury by a policy of calumny, plagiarism, and neglect, used against him by the little souls, of what was in many respects a little age, with no mercy and little intermission for many years.

Since the production of Blair's "Grave," he had been held up to public ridicule as an artist, in a paper called the "Examiner," edited by Leigh Hunt, and the occasion of this exhibition called forth another article in its columns full of crass misunderstanding of his aims and the superior sneers of a self-satisfied and material-minded writer. In it he was termed "an unfortunate lunatic whose personal unoffensiveness secures him from confinement."

But the "most unkindest cut of all" had been Cromek's, in making his own friend of thirty years' standing the supplanter of his work, the thief of his idea.

All these things had inflamed his tremulous and excitable nerves to a point beyond self-control.

Material disagreements of the kind I have related had a sad effect on him, and drove him to an expression of bitterness very difficult to reconcile with the benign, gentle and courteous nature to which all his friends and acquaintances have affectionately testified. There is no doubt that during the period of middle life he developed a hard and violent strain which did not mix with, diminish, or distemper the fine and beautiful qualities[Pg 43] of his heart and spirit, but shot through them like a barbed wire among a tangle of honeysuckle. In great part, it was the irritation of capricious and highly-strung nerves, the tension of an overheated and excitable brain, and not a quality of the mind or character at all.

The expression of this condition of Blake's must, therefore, be taken as an undisciplined and wilfully exaggerated statement of his intellectual convictions, with a deep note of truth at the bottom. It seems strange that in the matter of the "Pilgrimage" he did not go straight to Stothard and invite him to clear himself of the suspicions with which he regarded him. But like all guileless people, and perhaps especially those of the artistic temperament, when once they have been deceived they find it easy to believe that all the world is in league against them.

Before people who were not intimate, who were, in fact, antipathetic to him, Blake would abuse Stothard roundly and criticise him wantonly. But to the immediate circle of his personal friends or sympathisers—those who, knowing how he had suffered, and how black the case looked for Stothard, would have understood anything he might have said,—he maintained complete silence on the subject of the "Pilgrimage," and the name of the popular artist was mentioned without comment and listened to in grave silence by him. Once, many years after, he met Stothard at a dinner, and went up to him impulsively with outstretched hand. It was refused with coldness. Another time, hearing that Stothard was ill, Blake's heart softened and warmed to the old friend, and he rushed off impetuously to call and make up the quarrel in which he ever believed Stothard to have been the aggressor. But Stothard would not receive him, desired no reconciliation.

In the year 1808 Blake exhibited, for the fifth and last time, at the Royal Academy, two pictures in "fresco,"[Pg 44] "Christ in the Sepulchre guarded by Angels," and "Jacob's Dream." The engraving of Blake's "Canterbury Pilgrimage" was issued in October, 1810.

15

It was altogether unadvertised and unheralded, and the public held itself coldly aloof, neither admiring nor buying. The original picture was taken by the ever-faithful Mr. Butts. Stothard's picture was not finished engraving till a year or two later, for adverse fortunes overtook it. Lewis Schiavonetti died in the middle of the work, and another hand had to finish it. Notwithstanding all of which misadventures, it was one of the most popular engravings ever issued.

We shall compare the two compositions in a succeeding chapter.

[Pg 45]

CHAPTER IV
DECLINING YEARS

Seventeen years of quiet productiveness and unceasing work, marked by the increasing neglect of the world, were passed by Blake at 17, South Molton Street.

When finally abandoned by the public to the deep solitude which he created for himself in the midst of the roar of the city, the years are a record of much peaceful labour, of beautiful and strange work, produced as the result of his spiritual meditations and visions.

"That he should do great things for small wages," writes Mr. Swinburne, "was a condition of his life," and the poverty which had knocked at his door for almost half a century, now raised the latch and came in, to live with the Blakes as accustomed house-mate to the end. Mrs. Blake had often to remind him of the bare larder and purse by setting an empty plate before him, when he turned to his task-work of engraving to earn the needful money whereby they might live.

In the last years of his life Blake said significantly to Crabb Robinson, "I should be sorry if I had any earthly fame, for whatever natural glory a man has, is so much taken from his spiritual glory. I wish to do nothing for profit. I wish to live for art. I want nothing whatever. I am quite happy." And so indeed he was.

But he wrote in the Note-book these lines also, [Pg 46]indicative of the loneliness and misunderstanding of his whole life:

The Angel who presided at my birth,
Said, "Little creature formed for joy and mirth,
Go, Love, without the help of anything on earth."

The struggle between himself and the world being over, and his intractable genius relegated by the influential and great persons of his age to a limbo of neglect and contempt, then did he reach out his hands as to a friend, and pulled Poverty across the threshold; and stretching his limbs and shaking back his gray old head in relief and content, he settled in to the unhindered and undistracted contemplation of "those things which really are"—the eternal inner world of the imagination.

"They pity me," Blake said of Sir Thomas Lawrence and other popular artists of the day, "but 'tis they are the just objects of pity. I possess my visions and peace. They have bartered their birthright for a mess of pottage."

Gradually the ranks of Blake's old friends were thinned till but two remained, Fuseli and Flaxman, both of whom, however, died before him.

Johnson the bookseller died in 1809, in 1810 Ozias Humphrey; Mr. Butts, always a staunch friend, had no room in his house for more pictures, and fell off as a buyer; Hayley and Blake had long ceased to have a thought in common. Flaxman still continued to find engraving to be done by Blake, being determined that he should at least have money enough to live. Designing, which he would so far rather have done, was out of Flaxman's power to give, for the public had now sedulously turned its back on Blake. Much of this part of his life seems to have been lived in drudgery, but always cheerfully and happily. He was too poor to afford the outlay necessary for printing and [Pg 47]producing his books in the old wonderful way, and often made unsuccessful applications to regular publishers. "Well, it is published elsewhere," he would say quietly, "and beautifully bound."

Our artist had never been sympathetic to the decadent age of crumbling institutions and fallow literary and intellectual life that the last part of the eighteenth century presented; and now in the first years of a new century, a generation of new-born song, of enthusiastic lovers of liberty, of strong original and romantic minds, was to supplant the old artificial, social and literary ideals. Blake felt the pristine thrills of the great new birth in the poetry of Wordsworth, introduced to him by Mr. Crabb Robinson, and also in personal acquaintance with Coleridge, a genius somewhat akin to himself.

Mr. George Cumberland introduced Blake in 1818 to John Linnell, afterwards held high in honour and renown as one of England's greatest landscape painters. At that time he painted portraits for a living, and engraved them afterwards. In this work he got Blake to help him, and it was through him that the latter became acquainted with a younger generation of artists, among whom he soon made many congenial friends. Of John Linnell it must be recorded, that from this time forth till Blake's death, he occupied a quite unique relation to him, constituting himself the old man's chief stay and solace, and according him the attentions and the admiring love given by a son to a beloved father.

A new circle of friends and enthusiastic admirers, very young men for the most part, rose up around Blake, whose hearts, expanding in unison with the awakening life of the age, recognized in him a brother, a teacher, and inspired prophet. To them he showed his benign and childlike side, to them he talked, not in the old dogmatic sledge-hammer fashion, but in a spirit of rhapsodic revelation, of peaceful and joyous wisdom.

[Pg 48]As the years went by, a new fellowship with mankind, a large toleration and deep tenderness, bore golden fruit in his intercourse with this favoured band of young friends and disciples. As Walter Pater wrote of Michael Angelo, so might it be said of Blake, "This man, because the Gods loved him, lingered on to be of immense patriarchal age, till the sweetness it had taken so long to secrete in him was found at last. Out of the strong came forth sweetness, *ex forti dulcedo*."

Among the new friends were John Varley, the father of English water-colours, as he has been affectionately termed, Richter and Holmes, both leaders of the new school. These men were the forerunners of Turner, Copley-Fielding, De Wint, Cotman, Prout, David Cox and William Hunt, and though in these days they are little remembered, and the glory of them has been eclipsed by their great successors, their somewhat timid and delicate work in South Kensington Museum will repay a visit and establish their pioneer claims to our regard.

It was for John Varley that Blake drew the celebrated visionary heads, the only work of his with which he is associated by many people. Varley was by way of being an astrologer, and took the deepest interest in the occult and the spiritualistic. Blake's talk of visions, of the actual appearances vouchsafed him from the other world, had a significance to Varley's matter-of-fact mind much more vulgar and material than he intended.

Our artist had cultivated imagination till it became vision, and what he thought, that he saw, for, as Mr. Smetham wrote, "thought crystallized itself sharply into vision with him." So that when his friend asked him to draw the portraits of men long dead and gone, such as Edward III, William Wallace, Richard I, Wat Tyler, or unknown personages, such as "the man who built the Pyramids," or "the man who[Pg 49] taught Mr. B. painting in his dreams," and (most remarkable of all!) "the Ghost of a Flea," Blake had but to command his visionary faculty and summon before his gaze the desired sitters. The one which has been the most talked about is the Ghost of a Flea, and Varley gives the following description of the manner in which it sat for its portrait: "This spirit visited his (Blake's) imagination in such a figure as he never anticipated in an insect. As I was anxious to make the most correct investigation in my power of the truth of these visions, on hearing of this spiritual apparition of a flea, I asked him if he could draw for me the resemblance of what he saw. He instantly said, 'I see him now before me.' I therefore gave him paper and a pencil with which he drew the portrait.... I felt convinced by his mode of proceeding that he had a real image before him; for he left off and began on another part of the paper to make a separate drawing of the mouth of the flea, which, the spirit having opened, he was prevented from proceeding with the first sketch till he had closed it."

Various explanations of these portraits of "spectres" (as Varley has it) have been put forward. Messrs. Ellis and Yeats write of them, "All are pictorial expressions of personality, pictorial opinions, drawn, as Blake believed, from influences set going by the character of the men, and permanently affecting the atmosphere, finer than air or ether, into which his imagination looked for their lineaments."

A large and curious collection of these heads, executed by Blake at nocturnal sittings at Varley's house, is still in existence, but not in the British Museum, unfortunately. They mostly bear the date, August, 1820.

In 1820 Blake illustrated Thornton's "Virgil's Pastorals." These, along with his other art-work, will be[Pg 50] considered in a later portion of this book. They are the only woodcuts Blake ever made, and are unique, strong and suggestive as anything he ever did. In the same year he made a drawing of Laocoon, to illustrate an article in Rees' "Cyclopaedia" (to such hack-work as this he was frequently reduced to replenish the household purse). He went to the Academy Schools, and took his place humbly among the young men to draw from the cast of Laocoon there.

"What! you heer, Meesther Blake," said his old friend Fuseli; "we ought to come and learn of you, not you of us."

In 1821 Blake moved to No. 3, Fountain Court, in the Temple, his last dwelling-place on earth. It was at that time an old-fashioned respectable court, very quiet, though removed but a few paces from the bustling Strand. The two rooms on the first floor which the Blakes inhabited have been more graphically described than any other of Blake's homes. The front room had its walls covered with his pictures and served as a reception room for his friends, while the back room was living room, kitchen, sleeping apartment and studio all in one. One of his friends wrote, "There was a strange expansion and sensation of freedom in those two rooms, *very* seldom felt elsewhere"; while another, speaking of them to Blake's biographer Gilchrist, exclaimed, "Ah! that divine window!" It was there that Blake's working table was set, with a print of Albrecht Dürer's "Melancholia" beside it; and between a gap in the houses could be seen the river, with its endless suggestions, memories and "spiritual correspondences."

It is to the credit of the Royal Academy that in the year after Blake's last move, 1822, a grant of £25 was given to this least popular but greatest of her children.

Allan Cunningham and the fastidious Crabb Robinson give the impression that Blake lived in squalor at[Pg 51] the end, but the insinuation is refuted by all those who knew him well. Says one, "I never look upon him as an unfortunate man of genius. He knew every great man of his day, and had enough"; while one of the most attached of his friends and disciples (a young artist of the band I have mentioned, who attained success as a painter of "poetic landscape," Mr. Samuel Palmer) wrote to Gilchrist, "No, certainly,—whatever was in Blake's house, there was no squalor. Himself, his wife and his rooms, were clean and orderly; everything was in its place. His delightful working corner had its implements ready, tempting to the hand. The millionaire's upholsterer can furnish no enrichments like those of Blake's enchanted rooms."

It would seem that Blake, having won "those just rights as an artist and a man" for which he had striven with Hayley and Cromek in the old days, and having now established his claim to live as he pleased in honourable poverty for the sake of the imaginative life, gained a tardy recognition and respect among the intellectual spirits of the time during his last years. One of the friendly acquaintances of this period was Thomas Griffiths Wainwright, a strange character of great artistic capacity and sensibilities, and yet destined to be a secret poisoner and murderer. I wonder if Blake was thinking of him when he said in one of his conversations with Crabb Robinson, "I have never known a very bad man who had not something very good in him." Palmer Samuel has given a never-to-be-forgotten picture of Blake at the Academy looking at a picture of Wainwright's.

"While so many moments better worthy to remain are fled," wrote Palmer, "the caprice of memory presents me with the image of Blake looking up at Wainwright's picture; Blake in his plain black suit and *rather* broad-brimmed but not quakerish hat, standing[Pg 52] so quietly among all the dressed-up, rustling, swelling people, and myself thinking, 'How little you know *who* is among you!'" These few graphic and reverential words touch the heart by their simple directness and love, for to Samuel Palmer, Blake was "the Master." The names of Frederick Tatham the elder, and his son the sculptor must be appended to the tale of Blake's friends; Edward Calvert, who used to go long walks with Blake, made memorable by high conversation; F. O. Finch, a member of the old Water Colour Society; and the distinguished painter Richmond, who was a mere boy when he fell under the spell of the inspired old man. Blake showed this group of young men the most fatherly kindness, encouraged them to appeal to him for advice and counsel, and gathered them around him and talked to them simply, directly and earnestly, of his high and spiritual views on life and art. He poured his noble enthusiasm and other-worldliness into receptive hearts, and his words bore fruit in their works in after life. For this group learned from Blake that Art must express the spirit, and must interpret natural phenomena esoterically. Richmond tells the following characteristic story of how once, "finding his invention flag during a whole fortnight, he went to Blake, as was his wont, for some advice and comfort. He found him sitting at tea with his wife. He related his distress: how he felt deserted by the power of invention. To his astonishment, Blake turned to his wife suddenly and said, 'It is just so with us, is it not, for weeks together when the visions forsake us? What do we do then, Kate?' 'We kneel down and pray, Mr. Blake.'"

To these earnest young men Blake was as the prophet Ezekiel, and the home in Fountain Court got to be called by them significantly enough, "The House of the Interpreter."

Mr. Frederick Shields (who, like Blake and many[Pg 53] other great artists, will doubtless be honoured as he deserves to be when nothing further can touch him, and this world may not lay at his living feet its due meed of recognition and gratitude,) made a sketch of the sombre little living room in Fountain Court. His friend Dante Gabriel Rossetti was so profoundly touched on seeing it that he eased his heart in a sonnet:

| This | is | the | place. | Even | here | the | dauntless | soul, |
| The | unflinching | hand, | wrought | on; | till | in | that | nook, |

As on that very bed, his life partook
New birth and passed. Yon river's dusky shoal,
Whereto the close-built coiling lanes unroll,
Faced his work window, whence his eyes would stare,
Thought wandering, unto nought that met them there,
But to the unfettered irreversible goal.

This cupboard, Holy of Holies, held the cloud
Of his soul writ and limned; this other one,
His true wife's charge, full oft to their abode
Yielded for daily bread, the martyr's stone,
Ere yet their food might be that Bread alone,
The words now home-speech of the mouth of God.

The house in Fountain Court has been pulled down lately. The footprints of the great and gentle soul in his passage through this world to the "unfettered irreversible goal" have almost all disappeared in the dust and scurry of the last century. We can still think of him, and of those long rapt mornings he spent in our glorious Abbey. Full as it is—pent up and overflowing—with the associations of centuries, it will henceforth hold this one more—Blake worked there, Blake dreamed there, Blake caught inspiration from the enchanted forests of its aisles.

We may think of him, too, as standing in the Diploma Gallery of Burlington House, gazing with all his flaming spirit in his eyes at Marco d'Oggione's beautiful copy of Da Vinci's "Last Supper." Of the apostles he said,[Pg 54] "Every one of them save Judas looks as if he had conquered the natural man."

Mr. Linnell, always during this period Blake's truest, closest friend, introduced him to a rich and cultivated gentleman, a collector of pictures of the German school, a Mr. Aders, at whose table Blake met Crabb Robinson and Coleridge. Crabb Robinson thus describes our artist's appearance: "He has a most interesting appearance. He is now old—sixty-eight—pale, with a Socratic countenance, and an expression of great sweetness, though with something of languor about it, except when animated, and then he has about him an air of inspiration." Lamb was an habitué at the house also. Gotzenburger, the German painter, met Blake at Mr. Aders, and he declared on his return to Germany that he saw but three men of genius in England—Coleridge, Flaxman and Blake, and the greatest of these was Blake.

Much happy time was spent by the old man among the Linnell family at the painter's house, Collins Farm, at North End, Hampstead. Here he often went of a Saturday, and was always welcomed with keen delight by the children and glad affection by their parents. Mrs. Linnell sang his favourite Scotch songs to him, John Linnell talked to him of art and listened appreciatively to his wild poetic conversation. The latter made happy the last few years of his life by a commission to engrave a set of plates after water-colour drawings, already executed, illustrating the Book of Job.

The congeniality of this task, which was to result in the crowning achievement of his life, fired Blake to put his whole soul into the monumental inventions. Linnell also commissioned him to make a series of drawings from the "Divine Comedy." It is interesting to note that at sixty-seven Blake set to work and learned Italian, in order to read his author in the original. His[Pg 55] health had long been failing, and before the drawings were finished Death came to him like a friend who loved him, and took him from this cold and unsympathetic world (where, however, he had been strangely happy) to that other one, with which he had always had so close and mystical a communion. The review of his life, from a worldly point of view, is of one whose means were painfully straitened, whose genius was baffled and powers crippled, by poverty and want of encouragement; to whom the world's acknowledgement was lacking, and the fame of the painter and poet denied.

His own assessment of life, however, was very different. Gilchrist relates that a rich and influential lady (Mrs. Aders?) brought her little golden-haired daughter to see him. When this child was old she recalled the strangeness of the words said to her, a radiant spoilt child of fortune, by the poor shabby old man: "May God make this world as beautiful to you, my child, as it has been to me!" he said, stroking her golden curls.

I cannot forbear to quote from Gilchrist the passage which describes his death.

"The final leave-taking came which he had so often seen in vision; so often and with such child-like simple faith sung and designed. With the same intense high feeling he had depicted the 'Death of the Righteous Man,' he enacted it, serenely, joyously; for life and design and song were with him all pitched in one key, different expressions of one reality. No dissonances there! It happened on a Sunday, the 12th of August, 1827, nearly three months before completion of his seventieth year. On the day of his death ... he composed and uttered songs to his Maker so

19

sweetly to the ear of his Catherine, that, when she stood to hear him, he, looking upon her most affectionately, said, 'My beloved! they are not *mine*! No! they are *not* mine.'"

[Pg 56]The last things Blake did were to execute and colour the design of the "Ancient of Days" from the Europe for the young Mr. Tatham. When that was done, "his glance fell on his loving Kate.... As his eyes rested on the once-graceful form, thought of all she had been to him in these years filled the poet artist's mind. "Stay," he cried, "keep as you are! *you* have been ever an angel to me; I will draw you." And he made what Mr. Tatham describes as "a phrenzied sketch of some power, highly interesting, but not like."

In that plain back room where he had worked so contentedly he closed his eyes on this world, about six of a summer evening, to open them on the glorious visions of the next. Those beloved nervous hands which Mrs. Blake said she had never once seen idle, were laid to rest at last in the cold sleep of death.

The year of Blake's death, 1827, was that of Beethoven's. Of both of them it may be said that they were but strangers and sojourners here, and the language they spoke was the language of a far country. Catherine, the devoted wife, only survived her husband four years, during the whole of which time she felt his spiritual presence close to her. Blake, though so poor, left no single debt, and his MSS., pictures, and printed books realized sufficient to keep Mrs. Blake in comfort for those few years. John Linnell and Tatham piously cared for and tended their lost leader's widow. She died as Blake died, joyfully, and her body was laid to rest beside his in Bunhill Fields. There is no sign to-day to show where those graves lie, but it is as well.

"The vegetative earth" has absorbed the two dear bodies that the spirits of William Blake and his wife may shine the clearer; their bright radiance glimmers through the century like a guiding star, to lead men's thoughts out into the endless vistas of the infinite life which transcends our present limited consciousness.

[Pg 57]

CHAPTER V
HIS RELIGIOUS VIEWS

It seems to me that it would be quite vain and useless to go on to a review of Blake's art, and, incidentally, his poetry, without a preliminary examination—as concise as may be—of the fundamental religious and intellectual conceptions which made him the man he was, and gave him so strange and subjective a point of view. Blake is no ordinary painter, whose art-work is the only key to his inner life or to his perceptions of beauty in the natural world.

He is an artist and a poet of the highest spiritual order, but he is also a mystic. Messrs. Ellis and Yeats tell us that his rank as a mystic entitles him to far more admiration and patient study than any claims he may have as a mere painter and poet! Be that as it may (and some of us cannot but hold the artist as the most glorious manifestation of the divine on this earth!), it is certainly necessary to apprehend Blake the mystic before we can enter into the spirit of Blake the artist.

His was a strange religious creed. It is evident that in early life he obtained somehow or other many of the works of the great mystics and studied them with passionate attention. Among them Swedenborg (whom, however, he frequently criticised harshly) and Jacob Boehmen, the wonderful shoemaker of the sixteenth century, seem to have exerted the most lasting influence on his mind.

[Pg 58]Swedenborg's doctrine of correspondences—the theory that natural phenomena actually represent, or rather shadow, unseen spiritual conditions and existence—attracted Blake at first reading, and became so much a part of his mental fibre that one feels certain he would have eventually fought his intellectual way out into this channel of thought had Swedenborg never written. Nature seemed to Blake the confused and vague copy of something definite and perfect in "Imagination" or "Spirit." "All things exist in the human imagination," and "in every bosom a universe expands," he wrote, and in the human imagination and its reverend preservation and cultivation lay man's only source of divine illumination, he believed.

"If the doors of perception were cleansed, everything would appear to man as it is, infinite. For man has closed himself up till he sees all things through narrow chinks in his cavern," are illuminating words of his. Blake's whole effort in life seemed to be the cleansing and spiritualizing of the portals of the senses that he might see and hear and receive as much of the infinite spirit as his humanity could hold.

The mission which he put clearly before him always, he expressed in these words in his prophetic poem of "Jerusalem":

I rest not from my great task
To open the Eternal Worlds, to open the Immortal Eyes
Of Man inwards; into the Worlds of Thought, into Eternity
Ever expanding in the bosom of God, the Human Imagination.

No man ever sought more gallantly to batter down the walls of materialism which were closing round the souls of men, to let in the sweet breath of Spirit, and to unveil the Vision of the Universal Life. The immemorial struggle between the body and the soul of man was never lost sight of by him, though he sometimes seems to deny it, and his letters to Butts from[Pg 59] Felpham show something of his acute consciousness of the difficulty of subduing his spectre or "selfhood." "Nature and religion," he announces passionately, "are the fetters of Life." The orthodox narrow unspiritual religion of his time and all times was repugnant to Blake, and aroused all his fiery combative qualities. It seemed to him to be as actually a fetter to the spirit as the carnal nature of man. Religion was to him a matter of intuition, and not a question of creed or dogma at all. He gives a picture of ordinary religious conceptions in the poem called the "Everlasting Gospel":

The vision of Christ that thou dost see
Is my vision's greatest enemy.
Thine is the friend of all mankind;
Mine speaks in parables to the blind.
Thine loves the same world that mine hates,
Thy heaven-doors are my hell-gates.
Socrates taught what Miletus
Loathed as a nation's bitterest curse;
And Caiaphas was, in his own mind,
A benefactor to the Bible day and mankind.
Both read the Bible day and night;
But thou read'st black where I read white.

The last line is very significant of Blake. The world which made so decent and respectable a thing out of Christianity, which called success and opportunism the favour of God, and hailed the Prince of this world by the name of Christ, excited Blake's utmost antagonism. He announced definite counter doctrines on his part, and advocated in his vehemence, almost as partial a view of things, as in their own way, did the materialists of his time. "La vérité est dans une nuance," Renan has declared, but the swing of the pendulum of opinion must alternate from one extreme to the other before the precise "nuance" can be determined. Blake's noble but often impractical views have yet a practical utility, for only through a knowledge of the extreme,[Pg 60] can the mean be discriminated. Of his own personal religion it might be said that certain fantastic and strange tenets he *chose* to believe because they pleased him, as we may choose to believe in this or that section of the Catholic Church; but the most quintessential, intimate, and spiritual of his views were not beliefs at all, but simply and purely knowledge. He *knew*, by an intuition beyond reason, things outside the ken of ordinary men.

The deep melodies of the super-sensible universe reverberated through his soul, and he could never therefore think much of the hum and clamour of this material world. From this intuitive and rapt knowledge of the mystic there is no appeal, for it transcends human experience, and when Blake had it, he was prophet (teller of hidden things) indeed. But when he chose to believe and assert complex and sometimes contradictory doctrines, the affair is different, and we may give or withhold our intellectual sympathy as we will. In any case the spiritual and unorthodox creed which was the lamp of truth to this beautiful soul is worthy of deep reverence, but I cannot altogether agree with Messrs. Ellis and Yeats that a *consistent* basis of mysticism underlies Blake's writings. Even a system of mystic philosophy requires to be stated comprehensibly and in a recognizable literary form, and the prophetic books (in which the greater part of Blake's views are expressed) have no form nor sequence, and are as chaotic and dim as dreams. Messrs. Ellis and Yeats, it is true, have constructed an elaborate, imaginative and very coherent thought-structure out of Blake's prophetic writings, but owing to the looseness, confusion and unintelligible character of the greater part of the symbolic books themselves, the deftly woven web of mysticism which they present to us as Blake's does not carry conviction with it. It is suggestive, deeply sympathetic with [Pg 61]Blake—sometimes radiantly illuminating—but seems an independent treatise rather than an exposition. Deeply as all students of Blake must feel themselves indebted to Messrs. Ellis and Yeats for their learned work, and the real help it has afforded to a clearer view of his unique personality, I cannot but think that every man will—nay *must*—interpret Blake for himself. He was too erratic, too emotional, too much the artist, the apostle of discernment and the enemy of reason and science, to have constructed the closely-reasoned, carefully-articulated system of thought which they describe so graphically. Blake was an intuitive mystic, not a systematic or learned one. However, if Messrs. Ellis and Yeats have appreciated Blake's mysticism, in all its strange convolutions and cloudy gyrations, they have done so not by following his expressed thoughts but by stating from a sympathetic insight denied to others, what he himself left unexpressed. This does not materially concern the student of Blake's art and poetry, but it *does* deeply concern them that they should ascertain the *main* opinions which we know he held and the nature of the spiritual insight that obviously moulded his intellect, and hence his art.

He had a startlingly naïve and original mental perspective, and he focussed profound and virgin thought on Life, Spirit and Art. Virgin thought it was indeed, for tradition had little hold on him, and the social, political and intellectual movements of his time passed by him, washing round the rock on which he sat isolated, but leaving him almost untouched by their influence and atmosphere. He was never swept into the current of contemporary life, but was as removed from the London of his time as if his rooms had been an Alpine tower of silence, instead of being in the very heart and turmoil of the city.

He belonged to no particular age. We could never[Pg 62] think of him, for instance, like Rossetti or William Morris, as an exile from the middle ages who had fallen upon an uncongenial nineteenth century. He lived apart in a world of spirit, and concerned himself with the great elementary problems of all ages, bringing none of the bias or characteristic mental hamper of his generation to bear upon these considerations. His art necessarily ranges in the same primeval world, not yet thoroughly removed from chaos.

Mr. Swinburne, in his eloquent critical essay on Blake, finds him largely pantheistic in his views. There is something in Blake of the rapt indifference to externals, found in the Buddhist. Here is a characteristic assertion of his:

"God is in the lowest effects as well as in the highest causes. He is become a worm that he may nourish the weak. For let it be remembered that creation is God descending according to the weakness of man: our Lord is the Word of God, and everything on earth is the Word of God, and in its essence is *God.*" Here certainly speaks the pantheist.

From the study of Blake's writings the following points—and they are important to our future understanding of his art-work—stand out clearly defined. He believed in a great permeating unconditioned spirit—God—of whose nature men also partake, but subjected to the conditions and moral nature which result from sexual and generative humanity. And beside the unnameable supreme God there is another God, the creator Urizen, who is a sort of divine demon. He it is who has divided humanity into sexes, and inclosed the universal soul in separate bodies, and set up a code of morals which bears no relation to the supreme God, Who being altogether removed from, and above, the generative nature of man, does not Himself conform to "laws of restriction and forbidding."

[Pg 63]Urizen, who imprisons and torments conditioned humanity, is somehow subduable by this same humanity of his own invention, and Christ, the perfect man filled as full as may be with the Divine Spirit (for "a cup may not contain more than its capaciousness"), rises in the hearts of humanity, and effects its freedom, by aspiring past the Creator, to the Altogether Divine, and uniting with it.

Jehovah addressing Christ, as the highest type and flower of humanity, says to him, in the poem called the "Everlasting Gospel":

	If	thou	humblest	thyself	thou	humblest	me.
Thou	art	a	man:	God	is	no	more:
Thine	own	humanity	learn	to	adore,
For that is my spirit of life.

This makes us think of Blake's follower, Walt Whitman, who in the same sort of turgid and chaotic poetry in which Blake wrote the prophetic books, but with no mystic clouds to shroud the meaning, has consistently developed this thought: "One's self I sing, a simple separate person," and "none has begun to think how divine he himself is," etc.

In Blake's conversations with Crabb Robinson, this mystic view of Christ is very apparent. "On my asking," writes Mr. Robinson, "in what light he viewed the great questions of the duty of Jesus," he said, "He is the only God. But then," he added, "and so am I, and so are you."

Keeping this point in view,—Blake's belief in the identity of the Spirit of God behind all phenomena, the homogeneous character of the great creative Energy or Imagination expressing Itself through various forms and organisms,—another extract from Crabb Robinson's diary will help us still nearer home to Blake's point of view. He writes: "In the same tone, he said repeatedly, 'The Spirit told me.' I took occasion[Pg 64] to say, 'You express yourself as Socrates used to do. What resemblance do you suppose there is between your spirit and his?' 'The same as between our countenances.' He paused and added, 'I was Socrates,' and then, as if correcting

22

himself, 'a sort of brother. I must have had conversations with him. So I had with Jesus Christ. I have an obscure recollection of having been with both of them.' I suggested on philosophic grounds the impossibility of supposing an immortal being created an *a parte post* without an *a parte ante*. His eye brightened at this, and he fully concurred with me. 'To be sure, it is impossible. We are all co-existent with God, members of the Divine Body. We are all partakers of the Divine Nature.'"

The latter words seem as ordinary and orthodox as on first reading his assertion that he was Socrates seems wild and mad. But all Blake really meant (and I think Crabb Robinson only half took his meaning) was, that the vegetative universe being a mere shadow, so are the accidents of personality, the age one is born into, the organic form which incloses the spirit. So his personality and that of Socrates, their imprisonment in the "vegetative" life were differences of no account, being transitory. But he and Socrates were one (or at least related) at the point where their spirits (the eternal verity) touched, and melted each into the other.

He understood the Bible in its spiritual sense. As to the natural sense, "Voltaire was commissioned by God to expose that. I have had much intercourse with Voltaire, and he said to me, 'I blasphemed the Son of Man, and it shall be forgiven me, but they (the enemies of Voltaire) blasphemed the Holy Ghost in me, and it shall not be forgiven them.'" This affords an instance of the manner in which Blake intuitively probed beneath the appearance, and divined the spirit beneath, discarding the fact or body with which it clothed itself.[Pg 65] Another characteristic opinion of Blake's, and one that moulded much of his work, is the following:

"Without contraries is no progression. Attraction and Repulsion, Reason and Energy, Love and Hate, are necessary to human existence. From these contraries spring what the religious call Good and Evil. Good is the passive that obeys Reason. Evil is the active, springing from Energy. Good is Heaven, Evil is Hell."

"All Bibles or sacred codes have been the causes of the following errors:

"1. That man has two existing principles, viz., a Body and a Soul.

"2. That energy, called evil, is alone from the body, and that Heaven, called Good, is alone from the soul.

"3. That God will torment man in Eternity for following his energies. But the following contraries are true:

"1. Man has no Body distinct from Soul, for that called Body is a portion of Soul discerned by the five senses, the chief inlets of soul in this age.

"2. Energy is the only life, and is from the body, and reason is the bound or outward circumference of energy.

"3. Energy is eternal delight."

These postulates form links in a chain of thought, another progression of which is developed in "Jerusalem." Blake writes: "There is a limit of opaqueness and a limit of contraction in every individual man, and the limit of opaqueness is called Satan, and the limit of contraction is called Adam. But there is no limit of expansion, there is no limit of translucence in the bosom of man for ever from eternity to eternity." Certainly there was no limit in his own bosom, and in vision he expanded away from his own "ego" and merged in the universal life, the all-pervading Spirit. Opaqueness and contraction were the only forms of evil[Pg 66] he recognized, and these are negative rather than active qualities.

Indeed, Blake often seems to deny the existence of sin at all. Again referring to the invaluable record that Crabb Robinson has left of Blake—I quote always from Messrs. Ellis and Yeats' complete reprint of the part of the diary referring to him—"He allowed, indeed, that there are errors, mistakes, etc., and if these be evil, then there is evil. But these are only negations. He denied that the natural world is anything. It is all nothing, and Satan's empire is the empire of nothing."

In another place he writes: "Negations are not contraries. Contraries exist. But negations exist not; nor shall they ever be organized for ever and ever." Contraries, 'the marriage of Heaven and Hell,' seemed necessary and right to him, and the urge and recoil natural correlatives.

The great strife with Blake was always that between reason and imagination, experience and spiritual discernment.

The greater part of humanity seemed to him to see *with* the natural eye natural phenomena only. This was accordingly opaque to them, and did not let through the light of the Universal Spirit or Imagination, seen with which alone it was beautiful, as being then the symbol of something immeasureably greater than itself. Locke and Newton, the men of "single vision" as he called them, were the types of this part of humanity. He would fain have had men look *through* the eye at the infinite imagination which is the cause of phenomena.

23

As he states in a glorious passage in his prose essay of the Last Judgement: "Mental things are alone real: what is called corporeal nobody knows of; its dwelling-place is a fallacy, and its existence an imposture. Where is the existence out of mind, or thought? where is it but in the mind of a fool? Some people flatter themselves[Pg 67] that there will be no Last Judgement, and that bad art will be adopted, and mixed with good art—that error or experiment will make a part of truth—and they boast that it is its foundation. These people flatter themselves; I will not flatter them. Error is created, truth is eternal. Error or creation will be burnt up, and then, and not till then, truth or eternity will appear. It is burned up the moment men cease to behold it." (This is a mystical utterance, a spiritual discernment which will repay thoughtful consideration. It gives the Last Judgement—hitherto conceived of by the orthodox as a terribly material and mundane affair—an imaginative and esoteric significance very grateful and welcome to the spiritually sensitive.) "I assert for myself, that I do not behold the outward creation, and that to me it is hindrance and not action. 'What!' it will be questioned, 'when the sun rises, do you not see a round disc of fire, somewhat like a guinea?' Oh! no! no! I see an innumerable company of the heavenly host, crying: 'Holy, holy, holy is the Lord God Almighty.' I question not my corporeal eye, any more than I would question a window concerning a sight. I look through it, and not with it."

One of Blake's most beautiful conceptions of God is as the universal "Poetic Genius," and he was very fond of asserting that Art is Religion, which indeed it is when, like his own, it represents the forms of this world as the transparent media through which pulses the light of the universal Poetic Genius. Another belief of Blake's must be quoted before I leave this part of our subject: "Men are admitted into heaven, not because they have curbed and governed their passions, or have no passions, but because they have cultivated their understandings. The treasures of heaven are not negations of passion, but realities of intellect, from which all the passions emanate, uncurbed in their eternal glory.

[Pg 68]"The fool shall not enter into heaven, let him be ever so holy; holiness is not the price of entrance into heaven. Those who are cast out are all those who, having no passions of their own, because no intellect, have spent their lives in curbing and governing other people's by the various arts of poverty, and cruelty of all kinds. The modern Church crucifies Christ with the head downwards." And again, "Many persons, such as Paine and Voltaire, with some of the ancient Greeks, say: 'We will not converse concerning good and evil, we will live in Paradise and Liberty! You may do so in spirit, but not in the mortal body, as you pretend, till after the Last Judgment. For in Paradise they have no corporeal and mortal body: *that* originated with the Fall and was called Death, and cannot be removed but by a Last Judgment. While we are in the world of mortality, we must suffer—the whole Creation groans to be delivered....

"Forgiveness of sin is only at the judgment-seat of Jesus the Saviour, where the accuser is cast out, not because he sins, but because he torments the just, and makes them do what he condemns as sin, and what he knows is opposite to their own identity."

And now I must gather together all the frayed ends of this diffuse but necessary chapter, and put the vital points, around which the seeming incongruities and strangenesses of Blake's assertions arrange themselves, into a symmetrical if not an organic whole. The oneness of the Eternal Imagination, "Universal Poetic Genius," or God the Spirit, was the golden background to Blake's vision of life. And on this unity he saw contrasted the endless diversity of the spirit's expression in phenomena. All error (not sin, which he did not believe to exist) came from the fall of the spirit (through Urizen the creator) into division and the sexual and generative life of man. This tended to a[Pg 69] closing up of man into separate selfhoods, and each selfhood, in its effort to preserve its corporeal existence and separate character, was guilty of error, and gradually the inlets through which communication with the Universal Spirit was maintained became closed up, and were senses only available, in most men, for the uses of the natural world. This condition leads to spiritual negation, but is merely temporary, for when the body is destroyed at death, which is the Last Judgement, Urizen's power is broken, and the soul, however attenuated (as long as not altogether atrophied), returns to its pristine union with the Universal Spirit, and, though completely merged in it, yet in some wonderful way it preserves its own identity, or essential quality, while the body, which is error, is "burnt up." But even in the prison of the bodily life Humanity may be delivered from the cramping and negative effect of the selfhood, through Jesus Christ, who exists as the Human Divine in every heart, and who at the voice of the Universal Spirit rises from the grave of selfhood, and draws the Christian up into the life of that spirit where is no error nor negation.

It naturally follows that to Blake the one important point was to keep the senses, "the chief inlet of soul," perpetually cleansed and open, that he might descry the Great Reality of which Nature and all her phenomena are but a symbol or shadow.

In fact, Blake's hope for man lay in the contrary of Herbert Spencer's philosophy. The continuous evolution into new divisions and organisms, separate selfhoods and particles, was to him the falling of Urizen, head downwards, and bound with the snake of materiality, deeper and deeper into the abyss. By union, not division, by aspiring into the universal life, by conquering the selfhood and cleaving to the divine element (Jesus Christ) which exists in every human heart, Blake[Pg 70] conceived that man might, if he would, find salvation, true vision, and everlasting life. His own vision was always double or symbolic, and he prayed to be delivered from "single vision" and "Newton's sleep." For the preoccupation with Nature as an end in itself and an object worthy of study was to him the great error, a sign of the horror of great darkness that clouded the human intelligence.

In moments of a special inrush of spiritual apprehension his vision was "threefold," and sometimes "fourfold," which suggests that vista behind vista unrolled itself, revealing untellable truth and beauty to his keen etherealized sight.

These things, not being matters of common experience, must be received and understood intuitively, and not Blake himself can always make them comprehensible to us. His language and visions recall the language and visions of the Prophet Ezekiel, whose writings were read and re-read by him till they created a frenzy of excitement in his sensitive brain.

His opinion of women, far from being in accordance with our modern emancipated views, was somewhat oriental, though among his poems we may find many instances of sweet and spiritual femininity.

When Urizen created Man and walled him up in his separate organism with five senses, like five small chinks in a cavern to let in the outside light, he gave him a dual nature, male and female, so that he was at first a hermaphrodite. "The female portion of man trying to get the ascendency of the male portion caused inward strife," so a further subdivision occurred, and Man cast out his female portion, which became woman, and was a mere "emanation" of man. "There is no such thing in eternity as a female will," writes Blake oracularly, his happy experience being based doubtless on the beautiful subjection of Catherine Blake to his[Pg 71] own overmastering personality. Yet he is bound to exclaim in "Jerusalem," "What may man be? Who can tell? But what may woman be, to have power over man from cradle to corruptible grave." We may fairly say that the inferior shadowy nature which he imputes to woman was one of those opinions which he chose to adopt, though his real and unconscious belief regarding her was possibly very different. Be that as it may, he often makes her serve as a symbol for material existence, obviously an infelicitous parallel.

Having very briefly indicated the nature of Blake's religious and mystical opinions, it remains for us to say a word about his mythology.

In a letter written to Mr. Butts while Blake was at Felpham, these lines occur among some verses, and will I think help us:

For a double vision is always with me.
With my inward eye, 'tis an old man gray;
With my outward, a thistle across the way.

The personification and nomenclature of these double visions of his seem to suggest the genesis of this mythology. He has peopled a twilight mental world with a dim shadowy population of personified states and conditions. They bear strange mouth-filling names, such as Orc, Fuzon, Rintrah, Palamabron, Enitharmon, Oothoon and Ololon. What each symbolizes must be determined by the reader for himself. No explanation of their separate functions will be attempted in this book. Messrs. Ellis and Yeats have carried explanation and analytic criticism as far as it can be carried, and the reader who is interested in the literary matter of the prophetic books should consult their learned work as well as Mr. Swinburne's highly-suggestive critical essay.

[Pg 72]

CHAPTER VI
HIS MYSTICAL NATURE

To the world of his own time Blake appeared a mad visionary, whose sweet impulsive early poems attracted a few of the rarer souls of the age, but whose pictures and designs were practically unknown. His genius, atmosphere, and modes of thought were antipathetic to his age, and his aims and achievement proved so difficult to understand from the point of view of that day, that he was summarily and uncomprehendingly set down as mad.

This was an offhand and unintelligent method of accounting for so rare a spirit. The spectacle of a man who might, had he chosen, have enjoyed riches, honour, admiration and glory, but who instead, like his great Master, cared not at all for lordship in this world, but much for the preservation of the kingdom of the spirit that is not of this world, did a great deal to earn for Blake the name of madman. The world has always regarded the voluntarily poor with suspicion and misapprehension.

Then, again, Blake was one of those who lived very near the veil which shrouds the great unexplored spiritual forces. Death, as we know, seemed to him but the "passing from one room to another."

To raise the veil, to look forth on the cause of phenomena, on the visions of eternal imagination, to strain to the uttermost that he might hear the reverberations[Pg 73] of the unmeasured mighty stream of Divine power, to bathe within that stream, and let it bear him onward as it would—these were to him the real purposes of life, and being so, formed other reasons why the world, all engrossed as it is with wealth and position, and "here" and "now," looked at him askance.

To-day, however, there is an undercurrent of popular opinion—a small stream, but strong—that recognizes him for what he is, and his name is sacred as that of the great High Priest of Spiritual Art, to those who compose it.

It is noticeable that none of those who were personally acquainted with him, save perhaps Crabb Robinson, ever gave credence to the prevailing notion that he was mad: strongly do they condemn such a verdict. He was eccentric, abnormally developed on the spiritual side, and undisciplined in thought and speech. The mystic in him finally all but destroyed the poet, though it never arrested the magnificent development of his artistic genius. Again, much that is strange and difficult of apprehension in Blake may be traced to the fact that his mind lacked the firm basis, the just and right power of thinking, that comes from a sound education. As a matter of fact, capriciously self-educated as he was, his ignorance of ordinary rudimentary knowledge was as extraordinary as his acquaintance with much that is caviar to the ordinary intellect.

"Celui qui a l'imagination sans érudition a des ailes et n'a pas de pieds." And so it was with Blake. But it does not detract one iota from the illuminating quality of the thoughts which flash as it were from a heaven in his brain in times of creative inspiration. Blake on the wing has a strange beauty, a swift, direct and strenuous flight that thrills and awes the imaginative spectator. It is only when this wild wonderful creature is caught and entangled in theories and systems and human[Pg 74] reasoning, that we may not give him our intellectual adherence.

Other causes which appear to give colour to the theory that he was mad are the following: Blake had no curious regard or nice care for words, but used them at random in speech, just as they came to hand, and as he cherished numerous violent prejudices it naturally followed that he often expressed them in very emphatic and often unreasonable language. Passionate partisan as he was of the world of imagination as against the world of fact, he assumed an attitude of defiance to natural science and its oldest established facts which seemed to those who had not the key to Blake's mind simply insane or at the best puerile.

So accustomed was he to misunderstanding, that when strangers tried to draw him out he seems purposely to have indulged in exaggeration and symbolic language to baffle and mystify them. In ordinary intercourse, as in his art and poetry, he seems to have had no care to put his mind and his listeners or spectators en rapport with his own. That magical sympathy which some men know so well how to establish like a living current between their own and other minds before "speaking the truth that is in them," was not one of Blake's gifts. The sympathetic standpoint for observance or understanding he expected from those who would be at the pains to find out his meaning. "Let them that have ears, hear—if they can, and if they be not too tightly shut into their selfhoods, and their senses not clogged beyond cleansing with the dust and litter of materialism," he would seem to say.

Examining into the vexed question of Blake's visions, whether they were the apparitions of an unsound mind, the automatic picture-making of a vivid imagination, or the visual apprehension of supernatural appearances, we shall see that madness is not the key to them,[Pg 75] though we shall have to admit a certain want of balance and proportion in his intellectual life.

Sometimes one is tempted to think that he had eyes that saw the visible loveliness and manifest images in which Plato supposes that Ideas exist in the spiritual universe. Which being so, it is not wonderful that he was called mad, for the Greek philosopher himself said that "this is the most excellent of all forms of enthusiasm (or possession), and that the lover who has a share of this madness is called a lover of the beautiful." Our artist was a seer such as Plato meant, but his is a figurative rather than an actual description of the mental operations which suspend such visions before the prophet's eye.

All the writers on Blake—Allan Cunningham, Alexander Gilchrist, James Smetham, Mr. Swinburne, Mr. W. M. Rossetti, Messrs. Ellis and Yeats, Sir Richard Garnett—have discussed the subject, but I find the most illuminating passage in an article by James Smetham included in the second volume of Gilchrist's "Life," which I shall take leave to quote, for its matter could never be better stated: "Thought with Blake leaned largely to the side of imagery rather than to the side of organized philosophy, and we shall have to be on our guard, while reading the record of his views and opinions, against the dogmatism which was more frequently based on exalted fancies than on the rock of abiding reason and truth. The conceptive faculty working with a perception of facts singularly narrow and imperfect, projected every idea boldly into the sphere of the actual. What he *thought*, he *saw*, to all intents and purposes, and it was this sudden and sharp crystallization of inward notions into outward and visible signs which produced the impression on many beholders that reason was unseated.... We cannot but on the whole lean to the opinion that somewhere in the wonderful [Pg 76]compound of flesh and spirit, somewhere in those recesses where the one runs into the other, he was 'slightly touched,' and by so doing we shall save ourselves the necessity of attempting to defend certain phases of his work" (such as much of the literary part of the prophetic books) "while maintaining an unqualified admiration for the mass and manner of his thoughts." This seems a just opinion. The colloquialism "slightly touched" (just that and nothing but that) is the very phrase to express this elusive, almost indefinable condition of mind. In all mankind living in conditions of time and space, a certain adjustment of themselves to these conditions, and to each other, is a necessary function of existence. The failure to comply with such an adjustment was Blake's strength and weakness— the defect of his quality.

As I have said before, he firmly believed in his own inspiration, and with reason. For a mood of trance-like absorption would come upon him, his soul would be rapt in an ecstasy, he was disturbed by no impressions of earthly persons or surroundings, but was for the time being alone with his quickening vision. At such moments his mind's eye was but the retina on which God Himself projected the image. And he would permit no criticism, no questioning of work which seemed to him not his own, but produced through divine agency.

All creative genius must work in much the same way. The vision is granted, who shall say just how and whence, and its translation into any form of art must be accomplished by a power as it were outside, above, the artist. Vogl said of Schubert, that he composed in a state of clairvoyance. (That is the reason why the Unfinished Symphony was, and always will be, unfinished. Schubert transcribed the tormenting melody, the awful picture of Fate suddenly reaching a long arm[Pg 77] from out the smiling heaven to arrest the blithe jigging mortal so gaily tripping along a flowery path. The overwhelming terror and pity of it all shake the soul. But the vision was withdrawn, the clairvoyant condition left Schubert, and so he wrote no more.)

Blake's conceptions were projected in form instantaneously and with extraordinary vividness, and the vision seen with his mind's eye seldom varied or faded till he had transferred its likeness to paper. In this he was indeed unlike those artists who, having but a vague mental conception, build up their designs from without, laboriously selecting and copying, not that which will merely help to perfect the realization of the inward conception, but those things which they conjecture will arrange themselves most successfully in the making of an eye-pleasing picture. Such artists are but little concerned with the innate and obligatory form with which an idea must necessarily clothe itself. Blake writes in the Descriptive Catalogue, "A spirit and a vision are not, as the modern philosophy supposes, a cloudy vapour or a nothing: they are organized and minutely articulated beyond all that the mortal and perishing nature can produce. He who does not imagine in stronger and better lineaments, and in stronger and better light than his perishing and mortal eye can see, does not imagine at all."

At the same time in justice we must admit that Blake sometimes failed to make his vivid and living conceptions as clear to the world as he might have done, for the reason that he neglected to refer to Nature for the technique which after all is the language of Art. His art in this respect is somewhat like that of the Italian Trecenti, who uttered burning messages in a tongue which sometimes stammered. His impetuous soul never wholly achieved the mastery of material which only a prolonged and patient drudgery can give, but the images[Pg 78] which hurtled from his imagination were so forceful and superabundant that mere fiery creation, the unburdening of the overloaded heart and brain, was the crying obligation which forced him ever onward, seeking relief often in the mere act of projection.

It is always a wonder that he makes so few mistakes, his technique being manifestly deficient. When his drawing is right it is heroically, magnificently so, and even when incorrect, it is always of amazing power and almost convincing strength.

"Execution," says Blake, in his notes on Reynolds' "Discourses," "is the chariot of Genius," and when he mounts into the chariot and takes the reins into his strong nervous hands, then, indeed, nothing can withstand the flashing glory of his course.

At such times the affinity between our artist and Michael Angelo is very apparent. Both had the grand simple manner in their treatment of the human form, both worked as it would

27

seem "in a state of clairvoyance" and according to the direction of a divine daemon, both felt the body to be at best but the prison of the straining fluttering soul; but Blake's conceptions glow with a whiter flame of spiritual intensity than do those of the Florentine, greater as the latter was at all other points. I think it is the presence of this mystic fire which forms one of the great difficulties in the way of a facile understanding of his art-work. We feel ourselves in the presence of an incommunicable overburdening spiritual intensity. It has seldom happened that a mystic should be also an artist translating those things which transcend human experience into the terms of an art which by its very nature is only concerned with the sensible creation.

It is this incongruity between the thought and the language in which it is conveyed—Blake's thoughts often lying beyond the proper range of a graphic[Pg 79]embodiment—which creates one of the great difficulties in the way of our right apprehension of him.

A few of his works, as we shall presently see, are perfect and flawless as Art can make them, such as the "Songs of Innocence" and the majestic series of designs to Job. In both of these, the thoughts, and their incarnation in form, are harmoniously complementary each to the other. But often the thought will not, cannot be inclosed: it outstrips the reach of his art. Hence many designs are tumultuous with leaping ideas, dimly apprehended suggestions, not one of which is caught and contained in its essence, but seems rather, as it were, to flutter, tantalizingly enough, just beyond the grasp.

Blake "hitched his waggon to the stars," to use Emerson's expressive phrase, and to the spiritually "elect" in art—those to whom ideas are the really precious things—he speaks winged words and with authority. The pity is that his art speaks thus clearly to the "initiated" only. The sense of freedom of the spirit, of the absence of all contractile elements in Blake's work must however be obvious to all. It is his special charm, to be expansive, sublime, large. The great ethereal spaces of the sky have breathed their inspiration upon him, and he has reflected the colour and the mystery and the depth of the sea. To those who are spiritually homesick he comes as an emissary from beyond the Great Darkness, from where Life is found at its Source.

[Pg 80]

CHAPTER VII
HIS ART WORK

And now we must turn our attention to Blake's art-work—the fruit of his life "of beautiful purpose and warped power," as Ruskin calls it—and the expression of those strange thoughts, beliefs and visions, which were his real world. My purpose is, to turn over, as it were, the leaves of his books in the Print Room of the British Museum (the only copies available to the general public, though several finer are contained in private collections), and thus help to recall to the crowded mind of to-day's art the living burning spirit of Blake which is inclosed in those covers. After which we will pass on to a general description and review of his drawings, engravings and water-colours in the British Museum, and then consider his pictures in the National Gallery. A chapter will also be devoted to the Exhibition of Works of Blake which were on view for six weeks (January and February, 1904) at Messrs. Carfax's Rooms in Ryder Street, for this exhibition contained many of his finest works, and several which will not again be seen by the public for many a long day.

In Blake's time there was little hope of success for an artist who did not put himself under distinguished patronage and paint at the direction of some dilettante nobleman. According to the autobiography of B. R. Haydon the artist (a strange character if ever there were one!), who was in his heyday when Blake was a[Pg 81] very old man, nobody could expect to get on without a large dependence on patrons, who would often dictate subjects and treatment, and advance large sums to the painter, to meet his necessarily large expenses (for great canvases cost great sums); and on the strength of this, bind his creative imagination to the yoke of their own petty slavery.

Blake, however, being conscious of his own high mission in art, and deeply sensible of the divine obligation he was under to paint what he *must*, had to forego the idea of working out his designs in large, for he was too poor to pay for the necessary materials. Hence most of his work is executed in very small space—in the leaves of the books we are about to examine, and in water-colours and "frescoes" of very limited dimensions. As we proceed it will be noted over and over again that designs some six or seven inches square, and often less, are grand enough to be expanded into large compositions and gallery pictures—indeed they would gain considerably by so doing—for so much vitality and splendid strength seems cramped in a confined area.

But that *size* in pictures is no test of conceptive artistic genius needs no demonstration, though it may be conceded to be a gauge of executive ability. And it is in conception that Blake is pre-eminent.

Going quietly on in his chosen path, he has his little laugh at the crowd of artists scrambling like chickens around the patrons, who mete out the maize to this favourite Cochin or that admired bantam.

We find this doggerel in his Note-book:

O	dear	Mother	Outline,	of	wisdom	most	sage,
What's	the	first	part	of	painting?	she	said,	Patronage.
And	what	is	the	second,	to	please	and	engage,

She frowned like a fury and said, "Patronage."

Of patronage during his life Blake had but little, save from Mr. Butts, who, however, had nothing of the [Pg 82]conventional patron about him. He merely bought with reverent appreciation whatever Blake pleased to paint, never suggesting alterations or improvements, never blaming or criticising, but merely receiving in faith and love. For which Blake, as we know, "never ceased to honour him." But let no man think that poverty did not hamper Blake, though he chose it rather than the slavery that would have been the price he would have had to pay for even a moderate income. He himself writes in the Descriptive Catalogue: "Some people and not a few artists have asserted that the painter of this picture would not have done so well if he had been properly encouraged. Let those who think so reflect on the state of nations under poverty, and their incapability of art. Though art is above either, the argument is better for affluence than poverty *and though he would not have been a greater artist, yet he would have produced greater works of art in proportion to his means."*

Well, then: it was Blake's poverty and independence that caused him to work mainly on a small scale, and it was the fact that he was poet as well as artist—his poetry springing from the same creative impulse as his plastic art—that led him to merge the two gifts into a perfect union in the creation of his beautiful and unique books. The process by which they were executed is thus described by Gilchrist: "The verse was written and the designs and marginal embellishments outlined on the copper with an impervious liquid, probably the ordinary stopping-out varnish of engravers. Then all the white parts or lights, the remainder of the plate that is, were eaten away with aquafortis or other acid, so that the outline of letter and design was left prominent, as in stereotype. From these plates he printed off in any tint, yellow, brown, blue, required to be the prevailing or ground colour in his fac-similes; red he used for the letterpress. The page was then coloured[Pg 83] up by hand in imitation of the original drawing, with more or less variety of detail in the local hues." To read this account when one has seen the product is like pondering the receipt for a miracle. Gilchrist goes on to say, "He taught Mrs. Blake to take off the impressions with care and delicacy." After, they were done up in boards by her neat hands, "so that the poet and his wife did everything in making the book—writing, designing, printing, engraving—everything except manufacturing the paper: the very ink, or colour rather, they did make. Never before, surely, was a man so literally the author of his own book."

For the convenience of classifying in some sort of rough way, this chapter will deal with the "Songs of Innocence," the "Book of Thel," the "Gates of Paradise," the "Songs of Experience," also touching lightly on a very different book, Mary Wollstonecraft's "Tales for Children," illustrated by Blake.

The small octavo volume entitled the "Songs of Innocence"—with which the "Songs of Experience," produced some years later, are also bound—will be a revelation of beauty to all who have not seen it before, for there was nothing like it before, and there has been nothing like it since. The leaves of the Print Room copy, in all probability not a very early one, have become slightly yellowed with age, but the colours remain rare and delicate and iridescent as they were when they were first laid on, a happy accident, for this has not been the fate of all Blake's coloured prints.

"Every page has the smell of April," says Mr. Swinburne happily. Linger where you will, a gay and tender harmony pervades every leaf, the smile of an inspired child looks up at you and flashes something intuitive and precious into your soul. The colours are the colours of morning. The limpidness of the verses, the felicity of the designs, recall special morning moods in the[Pg 84] morning of life. Hope, innocence, joy, and an all-pervading sense of Divine nearness, are the characteristic notes sounded. Both the draught and the song weave themselves into a spell, each one distinct, each having its own charm, its own perfume.

The words without the embracing design, beautiful as they are, seem to lose some of that delicate and aromatic fragrance diffused from them. And the design without the words is an effect without a cause, and thus loses its expressiveness. It is the union of the two that makes the celestial singing, and, like antiphonal music, one part catches up, transforms and augments the

29

melody of the other, which, ringing silver clear, yet half-hid and half-announced its entire significance.

Our illustrations, in which perforce the colour is left out, are the palest, most spectral of shadows beside the glory of the original plates. They can but be reminders or suggestions, and must be accepted as such.

Plate 2, represents a Shepherd, pipe in hand, following a cherubic vision, his sheep in turn following him. The shepherd, be it remarked, has on a vestment peculiar to Blake. It is indicated only by a line round the ankles, wrists and neck, and a few rather realistic buttons, but it does not hide the muscles and the modeling of the body at all. It is a kind of glorified combination garment, but it is a matter of taste whether the shepherd would not look as well unclothed entirely. The garment, too much recalls the historic drawers which the outraged decency of the Vatican obliged Pontormo to paint on the figures of Michael Angelo's "Last Judgement" in the Sistine.

Whatever reason Blake may have had for investing his shepherd in this apparel, we are sure at least that it was not because he worried himself about propriety! such a concern was far indeed from him.

After all, this matter of the combination garment is[Pg 85] the merest quibble. The design has all the enchantment of the spring in its pale delicious tints, and the browsing sheep with the glint of gold on their fleeces bring something of Argonautic romance into this vision of April.

The flamboyant title-page of the "Songs of Innocence," is a fine piece of decorative design and colour.

The keynote of the whole scheme is set in the perfectly simple song, and the page in which it is embodied, called "The Introduction." The poem is written in brown, on a ground bright with tremulous colours which wane and wax in prismatic variation. Rose shoots, bent in and out, make a trellis up each side of the verses, and the result of the whole! well! you may call it a slight thing if you like, but it is as joyous as childhood, and strangely delightful! No songs ever written for children were as these songs; in especial, perhaps, "The Lamb," of which the simplicity and tenderness are of so delicate a quality that the poem cannot be handled critically at all. It can only be felt.

The slightly richer and deeper tones of colour, and the premonitory note of mysticism in the "Little Black Boy," afford a subtle charm:

And   we   are   put   on   earth   a   little   space
That   we   may   learn   to   bear   the   beams   of   love,
And   these   black   bodies   and   this   sun-burnt   face
Is but a cloud, and like a shady grove.

Who could have written this but Blake?

It is of lyrics such as this that Pater writes: "And the very perfection of such poetry often appears to depend, in part, on a certain suppression or vagueness of mere subject, so that the meaning reaches us through ways not distinctly traceable by the understanding, as in some of the most imaginative compositions of William Blake."

"The Divine Image" is another equally lovely poem,[Pg 86] with its sinuous growth of ribbon-like leaves, climbing among the verses. The unmistakeable figure of Christ at the root, raises a prostrate figure.

The verses, writ in golden brown, lie on a ground of palest blue, thrilling to Tyrian purple.

"Holy Thursday," after the rainbow tints of many of the pages and the luxuriance of their designs, is a Quaker-like and unpretending affair altogether. It would seem to be the untouched impression as it was first stereotyped off the plate; and is interesting for that reason.

There is hardly anything in the book more delicious than Plate 25, "Infant Joy." A typical (rather than botanically correct) flower with a flame-shaped bud, and a wind-tossed bloom, springs across a page dyed like a butterfly's wing. In the cloven blossom a mother and her small baby sit enthroned while an angel with wings like a "White Admiral" stands entranced before the happy child.

"I   have   no   name;
I   am   but   two   days   old."
What   shall   I   call   thee?
"I   happy   am,
Joy   is   my   name."
Sweet   joy   befall   thee.

Pretty   joy!

Sweet	joy	but	two	days	old.
Sweet	joy	I	call		thee:
Thou		dost			smile,
I	sing	the			while;

Sweet joy befall thee.

These are the spontaneous, gushing notes of the bird in springtime, careless, unstudied but felicitously right, not to be corrected or even touched, for each word must lie where it fell, just so and no other way.

Plate 20, "Night," with its graceful lady tree growing up beside the verses, is a beautiful shadowy design[Pg 87] on a background in which blue and green merge and deepen in a veil of evening mist and the poem is another of those minute pieces of perfection, which, like delicate sea-shells, were cast up out of the stormy ocean of Blake's mind.

In their own way, and with due regard to their special range and quality, the "Songs of Innocence" are the most perfect things Blake ever did, for he attempted no effect in song or design that his art was not adequate to express, and his imagination lies over all like the haze of spring sunshine. At that time the lyric poet in Blake was dominant, compelling him to sing, while the mystic was hardly yet consciously awake in him.

But in the next book, "The Book of Thel," the mystic has stirred and breathes through the poem. The story is veiled in a shining mystery, but is still quite intelligible and pellucid in style, till just at the end, when the sphinx riddle of this life, the paradox of the senses, the wonder and terror of death, close round the consciousness of Thel, and dark sayings are uttered darkly. Thel is the youngest of the daughters of the Seraphim, but is herself a mortal. All her joy in her own beauty and that of the natural world is destroyed by the thought that she must die, the flowers must fade, the cloud will melt away, everything must change and decay. The Lily of the Valley answers her gentle lamentation, telling her that in this very change, the feeding of the lives of others with our own life, lies the secret of an endless and blessed immortality. She herself will hereafter "flourish in eternal vales." Thel assents to this—

Thy breath doth	nourish the	innocent lamb: he	smells thy	milky	garments,
He crops	thy flowers,	while thou	sittest	smiling in	his face,

Wiping his mild and meekin mouth from all contagious taints.

That is all very well, she seems to say, *you* help to[Pg 88] revive and nourish many creatures, but what do I do? I shall fade away like a little shining cloud. The lily then calls down a cloud, which appears in the bright likeness of a radiant youth in mid-air. The cloud tells her that when he passes away in an hour's time, "It is to manifold life, to love, and peace and raptures holy." He will wed the Dew, and linked together in a golden band they will "bear food to all our tender flowers."

But Thel complains that she does nothing for any living thing,

Without	a	use	this	shining	woman	lived,

Or did she only live to be at death the food of worms.

Then the "cloud reclined upon his airy throne" tells her that even that would prove her of great use and blessing, for

Everything		that		lives

Lives not alone nor for itself,

and in token of the truth of what he says he calls the helpless worm, which appears to Thel as "an infant wrapped in the Lily's leaf."

This lowest form of created life is cradled in a mother's love to Thel's surprise. The Clod of Clay appears to comfort its weeping babe and tells the wondering "beauty of the Vales of Har," that being herself the meanest of all things, yet nevertheless she is the bride of Him "who loves the lowly," and is the mother of all his children.

Whereat Thel weeps to find life and love everywhere, even where she expected nothing but coldness and horror. Then "matron Clay," invites Thel to enter her house, saying that it is given free to enter and to return. So Thel entered into the secret regions of the grave, and passed on "till to her grave-plot she came and there she sat down, and heard a voice of sorrow"[Pg 89] speak from out it. It is a wild blood-stilling cry that rises to her terrified ears, shrieking of the senses, their limits, their precious and their poisoning gifts—these only avenues through which life may be enjoyed, and by which eternity must be coloured.

Nothing answers! there *is* no answer? It is the old Faust riddle that has occupied the minds of thinkers since the beginning of time. It fretted Blake into a state of painful excitement. "The Virgin started from her seat, and with a shriek fled back unhindered till she came into the Vales of Har."

The designs, of which there are but five, have still the serene and delicate air which belongs to Blake's youthful work. The colour is pure and thin, the outlines printed in faint Italian pink, and the effect of all is of things seen through a haze, which the sunshine is beginning to penetrate.

A delightful impression of rain-washed, wind-swept morning is given by the frontispiece, in which Thel—a motive of perfect poetic grace—contemplates the wooing of the fairy Dew, whose home is in the calyx of the flowers, by the Cloud. Above their heads is a patch of blue sky, across which the title is written, while birds and angels wing their happy flight in the ethereal expanse. Exquisite also is the pale vision of the lily of the valley bowing before Thel. And the cloud, and the clod of the earth bending over Baby Worm, are alive with Blake's peculiar quality of imagination. The tail-piece represents a serpent of pale green hue coiling and rearing across the page. One naked infant drives him with reins, while two more ride joyously upon his back.

About the same time Blake wrote a poem called "Tiriel," which will be found in the Aldine edition of his poetical works. It was never engraved in a book by him, and has little poetic beauty, being for the most[Pg 90] part full of clamorous rage, dire slaughterings and cruel revenge, but he made some water-colour drawings illustrating the text.

The Print Room does not possess a copy of the "Marriage of Heaven and Hell," which appeared in 1790, but the Reading Room has one which can be viewed in the large room set apart for rare books.

None of Blake's prose writings, in sustained thought and power, are equal to it. It is an armoury containing flashing rapiers, whose thrusts reach home as suddenly as they are withdrawn again. The glitter of steel in sunlight is suggested by many of its aphorisms. I cannot forbear quoting one or two, in reading which one would seem to hear the very voice of Blake:

"He whose face gives no light shall never become a star."

"The roaring of lions, the howling of wolves, the raging of the stormy sea, and the destructive sword, are portions of eternity too great for the eye of man."

"Prudence is a rich ugly old maid courted by Incapacity."

"He who desires but acts not, breeds pestilence."

"How do you know but ev'ry bird that cuts the airy way, Is an immense world of delight, clos'd by your senses five."

"Damn braces; bless relaxes."

"Sooner murder an infant in its cradle than nurse unacted desires."

"All deities reside in the human breast."

"Joys impregnate, sorrows bring forth."

"Everything possible to be believed is an image of truth."

"To create a little flower is the labour of ages."

"Improvement makes straight roads, but the crooked roads without improvement are roads of genius."

[Pg 91]The aphorisms are followed by five "Memorable Fancies," wild dreams full of paradoxes, and allegories both spiritual and grotesque. The designs to this book are very fine, but I cannot help thinking that this particular copy was not coloured by Blake's hand. In comparison with the one formerly belonging to Lord Crewe, which in all respects is magnificent, the Library copy is coloured too crudely, to be in the least characteristic of Blake. Particularly unlike him are the heavy gray shadows disfiguring the nude figures. There is no impasto work here as in the Crewe copy, but the colour is put on with no uncertain or unpractised hand, though in a manner unlike Blake. Far more delightful are the renderings of several of these plates as seen in the small "Book of Designs." They are worked up with the utmost care and finish, and the distinctive qualities of Blake's colour, the unmistakable impress of his hand, are there exhibited in their highest manifestations. The sense of mystery, innate to their conception, is preserved, nay, accentuated! whereas the Library copy, through its unpleasant, and I cannot but think un-Blakean passages of colour, has lost in some places this romantic and inimitable quality. The title-page alive with leaping flames, a nude woman bathing, salamander-like, in fire, the heaving body of a patterned water-snake writhing in foamy water, and a male figure seated on a mound prophetic of the design presently to be consummated in "Death's Door," are among the most notable of the pictures in the "Marriage of Heaven and Hell." Many of the pages are faintly tinted, while delicate suggestive ornaments cling about the writing.

In 1791 Blake designed and engraved for Johnson six plates to "Tales for Children," by Mary Wollstonecraft. The book is in the Print Room, somewhat yellow and musty. In no sense is it attractive, and it would find small favour with the modern child. The fact is[Pg 92] that Blake worked in dire constraint when illustrating homely scenes of actual life. He had no pleasure in the invention of accessories. In his art all is left out that may be, and the bare, the sparse, the elemental, and the austerely beautiful alone receive his attention, but always adjusted to meet the requirements of his own rigid sense of harmony in composition.

Then again single vision, "the vision of Bacon and Newton," concerned only with actual appearances, did not seem to him worth the transcribing. He could only work with freedom when the fact could be treated as merely the symbol of an idea. So that in these plates the homely domestic scenes he tries to represent have a cold and ghastly appearance. They are like nothing we have ever seen, because Blake was so curiously unobservant of details not interesting to him that he simply did not *know* about them when he came to draw them. His work is only of a high order when his imagination is excited. His spiritual insight not being called into play renders many of these engravings weak, dull and archaic-looking.

There are among them suggestions of the terrible, and of significances beyond this world however. They form grim and foreign accompaniments enough to the milk-and-water stories, and are about as suitable as the Orcagna frescoes in the Pisan Campo Santo would be to adorn the walls of a child's nursery. We willingly shut up the book and turn to one produced two years later called the "Gates of Paradise." The title-page says it was designed, engraved and published by Blake, but adds Johnson's name too. But we know that the book is all Blake, and it is probable that Johnson gave his name to the venture through a kindly, perhaps pitying, desire to help Blake with the public.

"The Gates of Paradise" it is called, though no glory of colour, no beautiful angels, no city of gold,[Pg 93] such as the title might lead us to expect, are displayed in its pages. Indeed, to some the first glance may bring disappointment.

These elemental and direct designs, sixteen in number, are very rough, even rudimentary, as engravings. But they are true art-work, for they concentrate and express conceptions and ideas of a rare order, and with a piercing directness that drives them home to our most intimate, most central consciousness.

Either you will feel their power and charm, and come under the subtle spell at once, or else you will glance through them unmoved, and perhaps contemptuously, and wonder what people can profess to see in this rude and Gothic draughtsmanship. If this latter is the case, then Blake has nothing to say to such an one, for it is no use to expect a literal and exact interpretation tacked on to all his designs. Blake must and will be discerned intuitively by his true lovers, and few words will suffice to indicate the track of his thoughts to such; to others, all the explanation in the world would never reveal him, for, to use his own phrase, "the doors of their perception" are not sufficiently cleansed to admit his conceptions.

The frontispiece gives us a reminiscence of Thel. A chrysalis, like a swaddled baby, lies on a leaf, while on the spray above a caterpillar—the emblem of motherhood—watches over it. Underneath is inscribed, significantly enough, the words, "What is man?" Blake's thoughts were never long away from this subject. To find an answer to the question was his deepest preoccupation and concern, and the following designs are all variations on this one dominant theme. Plate No. 1 represents a woman gathering babies like flowers from among the clustering ivy at the foot of a tree. In glad haste she plucks up one more to put with the others already lying, like St. Elizabeth's roses, in the[Pg 94] folds of her apron. The child is found symbolically at the root of what Mr. Swinburne thinks is the tree of physical life, embedded in the earth from which all things issue, and to which all things return. The next four plates are embodiments of the four elements, which in Blake's thoughts always teemed with "spiritual correspondences"—according to the Swedenborgian phrase. "Water" seems to be an emblem of folly and instability, and is embodied in the form of a man seated on the very roots of the tree of physical life, his feet set upon no firm earth, but upon the sand at the verge of the water. The foolish, helpless face, and hands spread out on knees, and the driving rain that descends with pitiless energy on all, go far to convey the idea of the perpetual flux and flow, the "unshapeableness" of the element "Water." A gnome-like man in a crevice represents "Earth." He is inclosed, bound down, weighted with clay. Sitting on a high white cloud amid the starry spaces of the sky, "Air" sits in form like a naked man, pressing his hands to his forehead in fear and giddiness at the vast immensity unrolled before his eyes.

"Blind in fire with shield and spear," a man strides in Plate 5. Is this fire an emblem of the fierce elemental fires of Desire and Hatred—both of which are blind?

Plate 6 is entitled "At length for hatching ripe he breaks the shell," and a delicious cherub having broken the egg proceeds to climb out of it into the sunlit air. Symbol of the material life which forms a concrete circumference around the soul of eternal man, the eggshell is broken, when "at length for hatching ripe," the veil of death is rent by the liberated spirit.

In Plate 7 and its successors Blake takes us back again to incidents characteristic of the life of man on earth.—"Alas!" exhibits a boy wantonly catching and killing bright little loves, which flutter across his path[Pg 95] like butterflies. Plate 8 is a youth throwing barbed darts at an old man who sits on ruins sword in hand.

33

> "My   son,   my   son,   thou   treatest   me
But as I have instructed thee,"

writes Blake, suggesting the numerous cases of friction and cruel offence which must result from the education of the human soul in selfishness and vainglory.

There is nothing in the series to equal the colossal daring of "I want, I want." Just a little cross-hatching, a little rough spluttering work with the burin, and we have this bit of marvellous irony. A group of tiny pigmies on a spit of land have reared an enormous ladder against the moon, and are about to start on their journey through star-bespread darkness to the pale crescent so far above them. Mr. Swinburne says that this was originally an ironical sketch satirizing the methods of Art study pursued by "amateurs and connoisseurs"—"scaling with ladders of logic the heaven of invention," and presuming to measure, reach and gauge the intangible ideal. But in this series Blake has expanded the meaning of the design into the passionate yearning and aching desire of man after things spiritual.

Plate 10 is a study of the sea. A water-colour in washes of Indian ink of very similar composition is in existence, and was on exhibition at Ryder Street in 1904. The water-colour evidently suggested by this plate is the finer work, but it is a marvellous evidence of Blake's power, that the tiny plate of the "Gates of Paradise" (1⅝ in. by 2 in. only in size) should be capable of representing so infinite a waste of stormy waters. One frantic arm reaches up to Heaven from out the foamy crest of the waves, a minute later to be submerged,—"In Time's ocean falling, drowned." That is its significance! No cries of "Help!" will be heard; Man *must* be overwhelmed by Time.

[Pg 96]In the eleventh plate an old man in spectacles ruthlessly clips the wings of a bright boy who wrestles and struggles under the cruel hands. Thus does Age, full of worldly experience and material philosophy, clip the wings of the aspiring soul of Youth.

Walled in by the divisions and materialisms into which Man has fallen through the creation of the generative nature, we see human souls despairing, and full of lassitude, enclosed in depths of icy dungeons, in the twelfth plate. This plate was afterwards taken as the basis of the design Blake made of Count Ugolino and his sons in the tower at Pisa in his Dante series.

In Plate 13 comes the promise of life. A man stretched on his bed with his family watching beside him, suddenly has a vision of "The Immortal Man that cannot die." After that all is different, and in Plate 14 "the traveller hasteth in the evening" of life to his journey's end, serenely cheerful, even anxious to shake off mortality, that he may realize his glorious vision the sooner.

But the way to Immortality is through the Gate of the Grave. So in Plate 15 we have the picture of Death's Door, to which our traveller has arrived at last. This early design embodying Blake's favourite conception was destined to be enlarged and sublimed into one of the most magnificent inventions of Christian Art. This is the first hint of the perfect final work, and on that account, as well as for its own intrinsic significance here, of the greatest interest.

Death's Door being opened, the Worm is seen at work in Plate 16. Who shall say how Blake has contrived to make the pale, hooded woman under the tree-roots so symbolic an image of the Worm? There is that about her at which the recoiling flesh shudders and sickens.

Yet here, below the dim, twisted roots of the Tree[Pg 97] of Physical Being, whence the embryo Man was plucked like a mandrake, is the house of the worm. "I have said to the worm, thou art my mother and my sister," quotes Blake enigmatically, beneath this leprous dream of mortality. But the enigma has a solution, for the worm at least destroys that body of generative and divided nature to which it is itself so nearly akin, and which has cramped and imprisoned eternal Man while on earth. So that we may be grateful to the worm in the end, for

> Weaving   to   dreams   the   sexual   strife,
And weeping over the web of life.

I have quoted an illuminating phrase here and there from the lines which Blake wrote and called the Keys of the Gates of Paradise. These, however, are but fugitive hints and thoughts suggested by the plates, and not in any real sense "keys" at all. Blake leaves each man to unlock the innermost mystery of those designs for himself. They are steeped all through in his own peculiar hues of thought, subjective to the very verge of the subjectivity allowable to art, but each of them exhibits that pictorial sense without which, however poetical and rare the meaning expressed, they could have no *raison d'être*—no artistic right to exist. They induce the mood which assists us to their sympathetic comprehension.

After the "Gates of Paradise," Blake began the production of the London "Prophetic Books," but we will consider these in the next chapter, and will conclude this early phase of Blake's work in book making by the consideration of the "Songs of Experience," which appeared in 1794—five years later than the "Songs of Innocence."

Again we take up the little book which was the first we handled in the Print Room, for the "Songs of Experience" are bound with the "Songs of Innocence." The[Pg 98] Museum copy bears the double title on the first page as well as the two separate ones, which occur appropriately before each book. Into this first plate, with its kindling title flashing across the page—"Songs of Innocence and Experience showing two contrary states of the human soul"—Blake has wrought some of that intense and passionate feeling which makes the work so valuable as much psychologically as artistically.

Two energetic and expressive figures, a male and a female, symbolize Innocence and Experience, while flames of Desire and Aspiration burn fiercely around them, leaping up to lick the letters of the title, which lie on a ground of flickering and fainting colour.

In the "Songs of Innocence," the marriage of the poems and designs was complete, and matter and form (poetic and artistic) attained an almost complete identity.

Here, however, the case is somewhat different, the task to be accomplished not being so easily achievable, for the mood is less lyrical and more mystic.

Experience is a hard teacher concerned only with this material life and its limited conditions, and sets itself against the Innocence which retains, in Plato's phrase, "recollections of things seen" by eternal man before generation here. Experience has nothing to do with vision, but only with facts, and it deals with the results of concrete experiment; never with the flashing spark of heaven-sent inspiration.

Thus the "Songs of Experience" are of far less simple mood and single utterance than their bright forerunners. Something of the remorselessness of experience has passed into these lyrics—for lyrics they still are, though Blake has lost the spontaneity and felicitous gush of melody which came from him so naturally, so rightly, six years previously.

Of one—not spontaneous certainly, but created little bit by little bit with unerring judgement and rich fancy,[Pg 99] struck out like the embossed design on a shield, each blow, each delicately graduated tap and touch, bringing out in clearer relief the magnificence of the heraldic images—of this poem, "The Tyger," it is impossible to speak too enthusiastically. It is a grand piece of chased metal work, and Blake has done nothing better. The fierce swift rhythm, imitative of the padding footfalls,

Tyger,   tyger,   burning   bright
In the forests of the night,

called out Lamb's critical admiration, and no one was ever better qualified than Lamb to appreciate our painter and poet. It is matter for regret that he came across so little of Blake's work in either kind, though we shall find him presently with something to say anent the engraving of the "Canterbury Pilgrimage."

One wishes (profanely no doubt) that our artist had seen fit to make the tiger that illustrates the British Museum copy, yellow and black, rather than blue and bistre and red, which colours seem to have no natural relation to the animal. Is it possible that this page was coloured by Mrs. Blake's hand in these weird parti-hues?

The "Songs of Experience" are pitted like a dark contrast against the sun-kissed radiance of the "Songs of Innocence."

One state of mind opposes itself aggressively against the contrary state of mind. One set of impressions is recorded in opposition to the impressions of sometimes the same things, sometimes their correlatives taken from a widely divergent stand-point. Thus the Lamb in the "Songs of Innocence" finds its contrast in the Tiger of the "Songs of Experience." Infant Joy is set against Infant Sorrow, the ordered beauty and sweetness of one Holy Thursday is the reverse of the despairing cry of pain uttered in the other Holy Thursday.[Pg 100] The Divine Image emits its celestial radiance against the cynical brilliance of the Human Abstract, and that other distorted Divine Image.

It is interesting to know that Blake issued the "Songs of Innocence and Experience" at the modest price of from thirty shillings to two guineas at first. Later in life he received four guineas for each copy, and during his last years Sir Thomas Lawrence insisted on paying twelve guineas and Sir Francis Chantrey twenty for copies.

At Messrs. Sotheby's sale of the Crewe Collection of Blake's works on March 31st of last year (1903) the price reached for a very perfect copy containing the four title-pages, was £300. The sum would have been wealth to Blake, but it is the world's way, consecrated now by immemorial tradition, to lay its laurels of reward and appreciation only at the *dead* feet of its great men.

CHAPTER VIII
THE PROPHETIC BOOKS

"The Prophets Isaiah and Ezekiel dined with me, and I asked them how they dared so roundly to assert, that God spoke to them, and whether they did not think at the time, that they would be misunderstood, and so be the cause of imposition?

"Isaiah answer'd. I saw no God nor heard any, in a finite organical perception; but my senses discover'd the infinite in everything, and as I was then persuaded and remain confirm'd; that the voice of honest indignation is the voice of God, I cared not for consequences but wrote." These words are quoted from one of Blake's "Memorable Fancies" in the "Marriage of Heaven and Hell," and in some such vein as that which Blake makes Isaiah describe, did he himself commence the writing of the "Prophetic Books." The sense of his great, though somewhat indefinite mission, came upon Blake gradually. Much of his time, even when engaged in designing, engraving and painting, was spent in thinking immense and original thoughts. They tyrannized over him, these thoughts, and instead of his guiding their sun-ward and most daring flight, they drew him along on their reckless course, sometimes bringing him to complete overthrow, as did the horses of Apollo when driven by Phaethon.

In the same "Memorable Fancy" from which I have already quoted, Blake continues, "Does a firm persuasion that a thing is so, make it so? He (Isaiah)[Pg 102]replied, All poets believe that it does, and in ages of imagination this firm persuasion moved mountains: but many are not capable of a firm persuasion of anything."

Blake, however, *was*. He had a fine contempt for argument and proof. Nothing mattered to him but the inner witness, the lively intuition of internal evidence. Convinced as he was of the cruelty of the fate that had chained eternal man into the bondage of the life of the senses and the division of the sexes; safe-guarding each self-hood from merging in the universal, by laws of restraint and prohibition, Blake took upon himself to proclaim a gospel of deliverance, to awaken man to the perception of the Infinite which lay without the clogged-up chinks of his senses.

He passionately advocated—Blake, the peaceful citizen, the faithful husband—the freedom of the senses, that all natural impulses should be enjoyed to the utmost limit and with the frankest delight. The body is but the accident of this life, and its free natural impulses may be trusted, for everything that tends to freedom belongs to eternal life, he thought.

Christ was the supreme Saviour, but to his eyes the Christ of orthodox religion was the God of this world, and therefore Christ needed to be held up again before men and exhibited as He really is, before He could be worshipped in truth.

And Jehovah was no other than Urizen, the cruel creator. In storm and excitement, in wrapt ecstasy and complete carelessness of consequence, Blake plunged into the sea of subjective mysticism, holding up from time to time out of the swaying waters lipped with raging foam, some treasure of thought, some broken image of speculative opinion for the world to gaze at. The pity is, that Blake who, in the "Songs of Innocence and Experience" and in his early poems, had so just, though instinctive and irrational, a sense of the relation[Pg 103] of poetic form to matter, as to weave his lyrics into "a unity of effect, like that of a single strain of music," should, in the "Prophetic Books" have suddenly lost, as it would seem, all perception of the claims of his subject-matter to any body of poetic form at all. The absence of almost all orderly sequence of thought, and this total disregard of the paramount artistic obligations of form, are the distinguishing characteristics of the mystic writings.

It must, however, be recorded in extenuation, that they were composed for the intrinsic benefit which Blake himself derived from their creation. Hints, symbols, rags of ideas set fluttering on the wind of his ever-inventive imagination, suggested so complete a sequence of thought and action to him, that he failed, in his passionate excitement and hot pursuit of them, to reflect that he had forgotten to state for our enlightenment that sequence which seemed to him so obvious. He was not concerned to make his ideas or visions intelligible to the world (the world must learn to decipher them for itself), for were they not fearfully intelligible to himself, absorbing all his life and consciousness?

Like a man intent and fixed before a vast and ever-moving pageant, he throws out a quick word of explanation, an occasional exclamation of enthusiasm, to the blindfolded world at his side. So present is the reality to his senses, that he feels only impatient with the dull creature which requires so much explanation and description. "I have told you, and you did not listen," he seems to say. But listen as we may, to the point of an anguished intensity, the marvellous Vision, Representation, mystic Something, which is being enacted before Blake, can, with the help of his jerky and disjointed speech, be but vaguely and painfully guessed at by us. Whatever virtue may reside in these dream-like books for the mystic and the occultist, their poetry[Pg 104] is not a winged and triumphant spirit any more, but a poor, wan, and halting creature, creeping painfully upon the earth on all fours. Swinburne writes on the subject with poetic eloquence: "To pluck

36

out the heart of Blake's mystery is a task which every man must be left to attempt for himself, for this prophet is certainly not 'easier to be played on than a pipe.'... The land lying before us bright with fiery blossom and fruit, musical with blowing branches and falling waters, is not to be seen or travelled in, save by help of such light as lies upon dissolving dreams, and dividing clouds. By moonrise, to the sound of wind at sunset, one may tread upon the limit of this land, and gather as with muffled apprehension, some soft remote sense of the singing of its birds, and flowering of its fields."

Let these gentle and appropriate words smooth the literary path of the "Prophetic Books" for all who intend to read them. It will be a difficult one for those who would study them seriously, even with the light shed by Mr. Swinburne's and Messrs. Ellis and Yeats' pioneer lanterns, for the road is rough and rock-bound, and shrouded, for the most part, in mist.

If we are forced to admit that in the prophecies Blake's power in the art of poetry was declining, we shall have, on the other hand, the satisfaction of seeing his art as draughtsman and colourist waxing in grandeur, freedom and nobility. More than ever in Blake's strangely sensitive pictorial temperament we find—to quote Pater's subtle phrase—that "all things whatever, all poetry, all ideas, however abstract or obscure, float up as visible scene or image." To many of his lovers, the "Prophetic Books" are among his most precious gifts to us, not for their intrinsic poetic value (which will be estimated in divers manners by divers persons), but as being the vehicle of his finest art. The first one we take up is the "Vision of the Daughters of Albion." (The[Pg 105] daughters of Albion, by the way, have little enough to do with the poem, their office being merely like that of a Greek chorus, to hear the woes of the heroine Oothoon and echo back her cries.) I am here referring to the one in the Print Room, though the Library possesses an almost equally beautiful copy. The book consists of eleven quarto pages, and appeared in 1793, just five years later than "Thel," to whose mysterious and delicate beauty it has a shadowy relationship. The thread of poetic suggestion running through it like a streak of sunlight is not so easy of following as the broad golden ray of "Thel." We are met at the very entrance by dim, unreal forms, with strange names—Oothoon, the shadowy female around whom the story centres, Theotormon, her jealous lover, and Bromion, a looming phantasmal personage, not definite enough to be terrible, though he is the evil genius of the piece. So now we are at last introduced to some of the personages of Blake's curious mythology. The argument—a page of the most delicate and energetic design, representing a radiant young woman "plucking Leutha's flower," which, in the form of a man, leaps from the blossom to her lips—contains in its two initial verses the clue to all the ensuing legend. Oothoon is, according to Mr. Swinburne, the spirit of the great western world, "born for freedom and rebellion, but half a slave and half a harlot." Leutha is the spirit of sensual impulse and indulgence.

Theotormon, to whom Oothoon wings her way across the seas, is the strong, enslaved, convention-bound spirit of Europe. On her way, Oothoon is ravished by Bromion, who appears to be merely brute strength personified, and the jealous and revengeful Theotormon binds them back to back in a cave by the sea, and sits down in utter wretchedness near by. All the rest of the piece is occupied by the mournful wailing of Oothoon, who desires to justify herself, and the sad answers of[Pg 106] Theotormon, which make a disquieting music like the wind among pine-trees.

Those who desire to know exactly what every vague phrase and unconnected thought may be ingeniously supposed to symbolize, must be referred to Messrs. Ellis and Yeats, who have possibly alighted on the real meaning and intention of these wild fancies. No system, not even that of the Zoas, ingenious as it is, seems quite to convince one that it is the ground plan of Blake's work. For my own part I shall not attempt systematic explanations of the "Prophetic Books," for which task, indeed, I am entirely unfitted, but shall merely reserve to myself the right of making suggestions as to possible meanings when they occur to me.

The beauty of the designs is the real glory of this and the following books.

The Argument and a very notable bit of decorative design and colour, representing the Eagle of Theotormon in the act of descending and tearing the beautiful, abandoned, white body of Oothoon, lying on a billowy cloud, should be specially noticed.

There is one extraordinarily fine plate worked in flat, even tints, representing Oothoon and Bromion bound back to back on the sea-shore, while Theotormon, with head buried in arms, sits on a rock above in the very abandon of stony grief. We have seen nothing of Blake's yet, so bold, decisive, nervous. The massive modelling of the Bromion torso is happily contrasted with the shrinking white slenderness of Oothoon. Beyond this passion-torn group, a calm sea, under a mild afternoon sun, shines deeply blue. We shall come across this plate again in the large book of designs in the Print Room. There, it is heavy and opaque in colouring, and totally different in mood, being gloomy and sinister in the highest degree. The blood-red sun hangs like a lamp in stormy purple clouds. The sea is deeply green.[Pg 107] All is ominous. Much more like this latter plate, in colour, than the one issued in the complete work in the Print Room, is another, printed off the same plate, of course, but laid on with an impasto. It was sold at Messrs. Hodgson's on January 14th, 1904, for £29. Neither it nor that in the "Book of Designs" is so beautiful as the one from which our illustration is taken. The plate in the Library copy is another variation, being soft, mysterious and pale in colour. The clarity and brilliance of the colour, however, must be seen to be appreciated, and this of course, our plate lacks. The writing and printed outlines of this book are in dead beech brown.

The next book appearing in this year, 1793, is entitled "America," a prophecy. It consists of eighteen plates. For richness of invention and design none of the books we have yet seen are equal to "America." The Print Room copy is printed in a dull blue, with a very happy effect, while the duplicate in the Library is in deep sombre green. Gilchrist says that no one who has not seen a coloured copy can judge of the beauty and splendour that adorn its pages. It is a difficult matter to see a coloured copy, as the only one definitely known to exist for many years was Lord Crewe's copy, which was sold last year at Sotheby's for £295. However, another coloured copy has appeared from the hitherto unknown collection of a lady in Scotland, and this I had the rare good luck to see before it was sold at Messrs. Hodgson's in January, 1904, for £207. Indeed it is beautiful, but with a quite other sort of beauty to that of the austere blue-printed copy in the Museum. The two are so different in mood and key as to seem like quite separate and distinct creations. Gilchrist says of the coloured copy which he saw—Lord Crewe's—that so fair and open were its pages, as to simulate an increase of light on the retina.

[Pg 108]That which I examined had the brightness and delicacy of Blake's colour in the earlier books, combined with the richness and grandeur of the later ones, but happily without the opacity and heaviness that sometimes accompany these later qualities.

Dürer's etching of "Melancholia" is the only thing in art to which the design on the first page of "America" may be likened, but, in Beethoven's words: "Es ist mehr Ausdruck der Empfindung als Malerei." A great winged giant or Titan, with his despondent head bowed on his knees, and his face utterly shrouded by falling hair, sits chained on the ramparts of the City of Night. Seated on a stone below is a beautiful undraped woman with a little naked child in her arms, and another leaning against her thigh. Heavy clouds roll up behind the genii and the ramparts. The mood of the picture is unutterable. The winged figure is red Orc, who will presently release himself and shatter the religions of Urizen, bringing fire and pestilence and famine in his train. He is Orc, the deliverer, but, like his great prototype, he comes not "to bring peace, but a sword."

In the wild clamorous poem Orc is described as the "serpent form'd who stands at the gate of Enitharmon to devour her children." Now Enitharmon is a vast mythic being without any defined personality; she symbolizes sometimes Space and sometimes Nature, while another facet of her various character, as we shall presently discover, is Pity. She is the mother of Orc, of whom, however, she is terrified, and the woman with the children in the frontispiece represents, I think, the same Enitharmon.

I cannot attempt to decipher the poem here. Before its roaring frenzy of excitement one is rendered dumb. There is no story properly so called. One merely gathers, that Orc releases himself in order to marry the shadowy daughter of Urthona,—Ah! shadowy indeed![Pg 109] After this, terrible things occur; in especial, that which may be supposed to symbolize the War of Independence between England and America. Whatever the prophecy contained in the poem, this much is clear, that Blake saw in the new world the home and harbinger of Freedom, the foe of spirit-crushing conventions, of shackling traditions and customs. Strangely do the names of Washington, Paine, and the King of England read in connection with "red Orc," "Enitharmon," and the mighty shadows of the Blakean mythology. With all his enthusiasm and patient sympathetic study even Mr. Swinburne has to admit of "America" that "it has more of thunder and less of lightning than former prophecies—more of sonorous cloud, and less of explicit fire."

But a far other verdict must be passed on the designs, of which our illustrations afford a very good idea, at least of the British Museum copy. From the first mysterious print to the last, every page is instinct with vigour and invention, and the disposition of the writing and the design on each page is in accordance with the most exacting and sensitive feeling for composition and decorative effect. Blake had the gift of decoration as Mozart had that of melody. He simply could not help being decorative, though preoccupation with decoration as an end in itself was a thing utterly foreign to his earnest and high artistic aims. In "America" Blake's outlines are put in with a thick strong line, a singularly happy method of expressing the bold designs. Plate 6, is specially interesting as being evidently his first feeling out after the top part of the design called Death's Door, which afterwards appeared in its perfected embodiment in Blair's "Grave." The lower part of the same design which we saw first in the "Gates of Paradise," is again repeated with differences in Plate 12 of the "America." The idea was a favourite one with[Pg 110] Blake, and in its various representations is always vigorously and poetically treated.

Plate 7, coming after so much that is alarming, exciting, or of sustained grandeur, comforts the eye and heart with its delicate pastoral tenderness.

A tree, with willowy bending sprays such as only Blake could draw, arches over a green sward, whereon a ram with woolly fleece and heraldically curly horns, lies sleeping. Beside him, on the grass, a naked child lies, relaxed in slumber, while another, cushioned on the ram's soft back, sleeps too, in joyous ease. In the coloured copy this page appeared particularly rich and satisfying. It has a brilliant iridescent background after the style of the first few pages of the "Songs of Innocence," but less vernal, more autumnal, in its richness of colour.

In what strange dreams did Blake see the pale woman of Plate 13 lying on the bed of ocean. Quick moving fishes flash around her body in the dim blue twilight, and a sea snake is coiled about her legs. On the top of the same page the body floating on waves is being torn by a vulture. Many of the plates are quivering with flames which shoot up in spiral tongues to play about the letters of the writing. Incidentally, the writing used in "America" is more fluent—running into dainty pennons and fluttering streamers of decoration—than any used before.

At the sale of Messrs. Hodgson's before mentioned, a single loose coloured plate of the frontispiece to "America" (Orc chained by the wrists) sold for £20 10s.

We close "America" regretfully, for a wild enchantment emanates from its pages, and entering into the spectator's mind makes him realize that indeed "everything possible to be believed is an image of truth."

In 1794 appeared "Europe, a prophecy." It has fifteen large plates, but before dwelling on them a word[Pg 111] must be said about the prophecy itself. The prelude is the lament of a nameless shadowy female, who rises from out the breast of Orc. She is also daughter to Enitharmon. Her complaint is often musical enough if we could but know what it was all about:

I wrap my turban of thick clouds around my lab'ring head,
And fold the sheety waters as a mantle round my limbs,
Yet the red sun and moon,
And all the overflowing stars, rain down prolific pains.

Blake would seem to have got fairly drunk with the excitement of wild words and musical phrases. There is little or no sequence of ideas, and the prophecy which follows the prelude comes storming forth, full of sonorous sound, but "without form and void."

All that can be made out from the din of frenetic words is that Enitharmon calls upon her son Orc, "the horrent demon," to arise and bring with him his brothers and sisters. But in the middle of her speech she falls into a primaeval doze of some eighteen hundred years. Patient and painstaking as the reader may be, an incident of this kind taxes his temper somewhat too severely, more especially as it seems a gratuitously irritating freak on Blake's part, without any apparent sense or reason to justify it. Persevering, we find that while she is asleep all kinds of dire affliction come upon the race of man, and the wild pelter of words and ideas hither and thither continues to increase in fury. It is like the dancing of the Dervishes—faster and faster, furious and more furious, higher and higher, so quick at last that the eye cannot follow the movements,—and then comes the breaking out of the wild demoniac cries, and the convulsive excitement, which is finally satisfied with nothing but the letting of blood.

After all this incoherent clash of words, full of "flames of Orc, howlings and hissings, shrieks and groans, and voices of despair," Enitharmon calmly[Pg 112]awakes, "nor knew that she had slept, and eighteen hundred years had fled," and proceeds with the roll call of her sons and daughters as if nothing had happened.

Rintrah, Palamabron, Elynittria Albion's Angel, Ethinthus, Manatha-Varcyon, Leutha, Antamon, Sotha, Thiralatha and Urizen are the names of some of the spectral shadows which pass before the spectator.

It is a dream of Walpurgis Nacht, obscure and vague; its warrings being no more than the dissolving shadows of fighting men partially discerned on a dark wall.

But if Blake can no longer take us with him into the infinite on the wings of his poetry, he can with his pencil create on a sheet of paper a world of imagination, which in relation to this actual world is evanescent and to some impalpable. But Blake's magic has caught and held it, as Peleus caught and held the silver-footed Thetis, though she changed from one form to another hoping to frighten him into letting her go, till tired of his persistence she revealed herself to him in her own wondrous form. Even so, Blake caught and held that which his imagination discriminated, undismayed by conditions which cause some men's heads to reel, until he succeeded in committing it to outline and colour.

The first plate represents "The Ancient of Days setting a compass upon the face of the earth." (See Proverbs, viii. 27.) The Museum copy has a passage from "Paradise Lost" written, or rather scrawled, in black ink underneath the picture. One wonders whose could have been the irreverent pen to deface in this way a page of the Master's work. The design itself is one of the finest that ever came from Blake's hand. The thing is tremendous! Involuntarily the mind seeks for its like only on the roof of the Sistine. Blake's art owns no master, links itself to no predecessor, save Michael Angelo.

[Pg 113]This was the last design to be repeated by his hand. On his deathbed he executed it for his young friend Mr. Tatham. The latter refers to the incident in a letter published in 1803, in the "Rossetti Papers":

"The Ancient of Days with the compasses was the subject that Blake finished for me on his deathbed. He threw it down and said, 'There, I hope Mr. Tatham will like it,' and then said, 'Kate, I will draw your portrait; you have been a good wife to me.' And he made a frenzied sketch of her, which, when done, he sang himself joyously and most happily—literally with songs—into the arms of the grim enemy, and yielded up his sweet spirit."

The conception is of sublimity and boldness, and in the execution of this particular plate the colour is laid on with great care, being shaded and stippled to a high degree of finish. The attitude of the Architect of the Universe is heroic, and is characteristic of Blake in his best manner. Leaning far out from the centre of the sun itself, a grand male figure, with hair and beard streaming in the wind of cosmic motion, measures the space below him with a compass, indicating the orbit on which the world is to travel.

The Museum possesses another edition, as a separate drawing, in one of the portfolios, which we shall examine later. Mr. Sydney Morse possesses yet another, which was on view at Messrs. Carfax's Gallery; and a fourth, probably the finest of all these different renderings, was sold with the title-page and three plates of "Europe," at Messrs. Hodgson's sale for £80.

The frontispiece to "Europe" has a magnificent evil-looking snake on the centre of the page, blue hills and distance seen through its mottled coils.

"The Pilgrim," some verses by Ann Radcliffe, are scrawled on the blank reverse of the leaf. The first and last time it may be supposed that Ann Radcliffe[Pg 114]found herself in such august company! All of the plates in this book are defaced by the same handwriting.

Blake's writing and the engraved outlines are of a bluish green colour.

"Red Orc" is seen in the second plate climbing up the sky and about to take his station on a bank of cloud outlined boldly against the blue. Below him, in a limbo of darkness, three naked passions in the form of demons are struggling together and falling down into the nether heavens.

On the page entitled "a Prophecy" a lovely angel takes her despairing flight through the sky. Her wings merge from white and mauve to a deep blue like that of a pigeon's neck, her beautiful feet gleam white against the rosy cloud behind, and her hair falls over her face in abandon of grief or fear or despair—we know not which. All the different and delicate shades in an hydrangea are to be found in this plate, and would seem to have suggested its subtle colour harmonies.

For pure melody of line the next plate surpasses it, however. Enitharmon, fierce, beautiful, nude, descends in a cloud to awaken Orc, who lies face downward on the earth, the outline of his figure suggesting a young love-god rather than the fierce personality of the terrible Orc. Even the flames about his head might be those of love. The colour is very delicate and transparent.

Then follow two full-page interiors, which, in spite of the fine drawing and colour, oppress, with the uncomfortable sensation of confinement, airlessness! The fact is, that we are so accustomed to Blake's open air windy wilds, and broad spaces of sky and cloud, that we do not feel at home with him when he takes us within doors.

Another plate from the "Europe," the lines of which we reproduce, represents two lithe nude women springing upwards with incomparable grace and the true Blake[Pg 115] vigour, among arching wheat stems. They blow horns through which descends a fall of blight upon the corn. The decorative rightness, the exquisite appreciation of the melodies of form, the vitality of action, cannot be too much admired. And the colour! The tender flesh-painting contrasted with the young green of the corn!—Yet Mr. Swinburne, usually so intensely alive to the beautiful, and especially Blake's beautiful, describes the plate in these terms: "Mildews are seen incarnate as foul, flushed women with strenuous limbs contorted, blighting ears of corn with the violent breath of their inflated mouths."

There is some delicate tracery of cobwebs, among leaves and greenery, on another page, exhibiting Blake in a marvellously naturalistic mood for once, and a final plate of a man rescuing a woman and child from fierce, rolling flames. No one ever painted fire as Blake did, and over and over again in his treatment of this favourite motive we shall have to own that he is, as Mr. William Michael Rossetti says, in this respect at least, "supreme painter."

As I do not know where to place the tiny book or pamphlet entitled, "There is no Natural Religion,"—it having no date affixed to it,—I shall refer to it here. It consists of eleven illustrated leaves, each containing in the engraved text a didactic statement or thesis by Blake on this favourite subject. Below the words, which give much illumination to his peculiar opinions, are small, rough drawings made with a brush full of heavy black, relieved in parts by outlines in sepia.

CHAPTER IX
THE PROPHETIC BOOKS CONTINUED

In studying the next book which Blake produced in 1794—the "Book of Urizen"—it is necessary to disabuse our minds of the idea that Blake's thoughts were not clear to himself. However confused and troubled they appear to us, they were certainly clear as sunlight to him, but he failed in the labour of reducing them to terms of intellectual definiteness, much less to terms of poetic art. The excitement which these visions brought upon his tremulous and sensitive brain seems to have induced a kind of "possession," similar to that of the maenads at the festival of Dionysus of old, so that no very consecutive utterance may be expected from him. Yet there *is* a kind of sequence in "Urizen," and the marvellous illustrations to the book cannot be properly appreciated without holding the thread of the so-called poem. Setting aside the ancient Biblical tradition, our prophet undertakes no less a task than the writing of a new Genesis, which in its naked horror and despair causes the very gods themselves to hide their faces out of pity to the sons of men.

Urizen the creator, the god of restraints and prohibitions, becomes self-inclosed and divides himself from Eternity and the Eternals.

In fire and strife and anguish he creates the world, "like a black globe, viewed by the Sons of Eternity, standing on the shore of the Infinite Ocean, like a human heart struggling and beating, the vast world of Urizen[Pg 117] appears." But after this effort he is laid in "stony sleep unorganized rent from eternity." Los, who is Time, was then wrenched out of Urizen, and suffers fierce pain in the act of separation and division. Then, while Time works with hammers at his forge, fires belching around, he sees, nay! appears to assist at, the further changes of Urizen. For the "formless god" is gradually taking form, and inclosing himself in a human body. He assumes bones, heart, brain, eyes, ears, nostrils, stomach, throat, tongue, arms, legs, and feet. And now "his eternal life like a dream was obliterated." An age of intense agony and stress was allotted to the evolution and development of each created portion of the body.

Meanwhile Los "forged chains new and new, numbering with links, hours, days and years."

When Los had finished his unwilling task, and saw Urizen all bound with the chains of time, the senses, and the enclosing boundaries of his own selfhood, "Pity began." This is another painful division and shrinkage,—

In tears and cries imbodied
A female form trembling and pale,
Waves before his deathy face.

Her name is Pity or Enitharmon. She is also Space, and her union with Los or Time naturally follows. The Eternals are so terrified at what Urizen has done, that they enclose the new creation in a tent to hide it from their sight, and call the tent Science. From the union of Space and Time springs a child, Orc, hereafter the deliverer, whom the father and mother chain with the chain of jealousy below the deathful shadow of Urizen.

Urizen then explores his new kingdom, and, looking on his teeming world, he sickened, for he saw "that no flesh nor spirit could keep his iron laws (of prohibition and restraint) one moment." So he made a great Web[Pg 118] or Net, and flung it over all, and this was called the Net of Religion. And of his now finished Creation it is written,

41

Six	days	they		shrunk	up	from	existence
And	on	the		seventh	day	they	rested.
And	they	blessed	the	seventh	day	in	sick	hope,

And forgot their eternal life.

The evolution or changes of Urizen form the subjects of a great number of the plates. Blake has wrought here through the pictorial medium as Dante wrought the "Inferno" in his own art. The same high imagination, the same passionate and unshrinking realization of it, the same terrible force are integral parts of the minds of both artists, and inspire both works, different in kind as they are and separated by centuries of thought and feeling. No wonder that Linnell desired Blake in his old age to make drawings from the "Inferno," "thinking him the very man and only to illustrate Dante."

The prelude to the book is set in a tender and lovely key, very difficult, however, to harmonize with what follows. It is not obvious why it occurs here or what connection it has with the dark story of Urizen. The same little picture will be found in the smaller Book of Designs, but there it is quite differently rendered as to colour, and I think more beautifully. Our reproduction is from the latter plate.

The cloud-like form of a beautiful woman, drifts across the sky, drawing by the hand a little baby, with the ideal face of sweet infancy. There is a delicious curve in the woman's body, a swirl of the garments, and a quick, fish-like, darting movement about the action of the child which contribute to the impression of flight through a buoyant atmosphere.

Turning over the pages of "Urizen" one terror after another takes the breath and quickens the pulse. Urizen—or is it Orc?—his terrible face averted, strides[Pg 119]through a world of fire dividing the flames with his arms.

A human figure, snake-encircled, falls headlong into raging flames, recalling a somewhat similar idea in "America." Los is next seen, howling in fire, because of his painful separation from Urizen.

Poor solitary thinker! what shuddering emotions must have rent Blake as his relentless hand drew and coloured the visionary appearances of these monsters of imagination!

To the hot and lurid impression of Plate 6 succeeds one, in which a pallid skeleton, bowed head between knees, sits grisly on the ground. Urizen assumes bones. In much the same attitude, but now turned to the spectator, the next plate shows us an arresting figure. An old man, nude, with white hair, and patriarchal beard sweeping the ground, shows an upturned despairing blind face. Suggestions of indescribable suffering are incarnate in this design. I shall take the liberty of calling the type the "Blake old man." We come across it again and again, and it instances his tendency to concentrate all varieties into a type, to make his artistic language as bare and simple and elemental as possible.

The story can be traced through all the plates. Urizen visiting his new world forms a series of six wonderful plates, of which one is very Gothic, representing as it does an amphibious-looking old man very like a gargoyle sinking slowly through a world of water. It is a true grotesque.

The most poetic of all the pictures is, I think, the one which represents the Birth of Enitharmon or Pity. Rising from a cloudy abyss with that bubble-like buoyancy which Blake knew so well how to breathe into his figures, a nude woman with body bowed in anguish floats upward. The face, with its strange dim, tortured eyes, speaks of the suffering which only the complex[Pg 120] and self-conscious soul born of the mingled forces that produced the French Revolution and the New Age is capable of experiencing. The body is of wonderful beauty and purity. On the brink of the abyss from which she rises like the smoke of a hidden fire, Los kneels with head bowed in arms. His deep musings have brought forth this strange sorrow-laden beauty.

Another picture, Humanity chained by the wrists and ankles in slavery, its blind eyes raining tears, but with the light of Eternity like an aureole behind its head, is seen waiting, waiting, with an endless and most painful patience, for some final deliverance. Like Michael Angelo's "Il Penseroso," "it fascinates and is intolerable." No more piteous or significant symbol of humanity has ever been conceived, in the full compass of its sorrow, its slavery, and its hope. Blake utters a Promethean cry in "Urizen." He calls out on the creator for having imprisoned and tormented us. A wild ineffectual cry enough, and one not consistent with brighter and saner views, which he held as passionately, but then,—it is Blake! And Blake was never able "to build a house large enough for his ideas." The Print Room does not contain a copy of the "Book of Ahania" which is a continuation of the theme of "Urizen," but short and unillustrated.

The small Book of Designs should be looked at in conjunction with "Thel," "Urizen," the "Daughters of Albion" and the "Marriage of Heaven and Hell," for the plates are repetitions from these books often far more rich in colour and delicate in execution than those in the complete works.

The large Book of Designs contains, among many plates familiar in design to us, though varied always in colouring, four, which we have not seen before, and can see nowhere else. The first is a colour-print of morning or Glad Day. It is a radiant design, but like many[Pg 121] of these colour-prints of Blake, somewhat the worse for time, having the paint rubbed off and blackened in parts. Blake's colour-printing process was as follows, according to the only extant account:

He drew the outline heavily in chalk on a mill-board and put on the colour diluted with oil or glue in thick patches, and printed the wet impression off on to paper. He then worked upon this rough ground, when dry, in water colour. But only in a few instances did he show complete mastery of the ingenious method.

The second plate I would call attention to is a nightmare horror entitled the "Accusers of Theft, Adultery and Murder." There are a trio of furies, only male instead of female; the watermark of the paper is 1794. A similar design, not so finely coloured, was sold at Messrs. Hodgson's for £15 10s. The third is a lovely little gem representing John the Baptist preaching to a beautifully grouped crowd. Its fellow sold at the same sale for £26 10s. The fourth represents a semi-nude figure, with head downcast, sitting beneath the bent and blasted stump of a tree, while to the left a woman nude and of remarkable beauty tosses a child high in arm. It is thought that this plate may have been intended for a cancel in "America"; for another one, more beautiful in colouring than this, which was also sold at Messrs. Hodgson's, and for £42, was found to bear some text from "America," faintly discernible under the colouring on the upper half of the plate, which could be read only from the back.

In 1795 Blake produced the "Song of Los." The Print Room copy is heavy and opaque in colour, though very splendid and rich, and the Library copy is similar in most respects. It was evidently colour-printed after the method described above, for the peculiar mottled backgrounds are an effect that could not very well have been realized by any other method, nor even then are[Pg 122] they understandable, unless indeed Blake had a wooden stamp which he impressed on the blobs of colour first laid on the paper itself.

The "Song of Los" is the Song of Time, and includes the "Songs of Africa, and Asia." So now Blake has written a song of prophecy for each of the four great parts of the earth. "Africa" deals in a wild incoherent way with the rise of the various religions. Urizen delivers his laws of brass and iron and gold to all the Nations. These were "the nets and gins and traps to clutch the joys of Eternity," and Har and Heva—representatives of natural humanity—find "all the vast of Nature shrunk before their shrunken eyes," for the senses are the limits put upon perception.

Thus the terrible race of Los and Enitharmon gave
Laws and Religions to the Sons of Har, binding them more
And more to Earth: closing and restraining:
Till a philosophy of the Five Senses was complete.
Urizen wept and gave it into the hands of Newton and Locke!

In "Asia" Urizen hears the despairing cry of his creation, and himself shudders and weeps, but unavailingly. Orc is heard raging on Mount Atlas, where he is chained down with the chain of jealousy. Orc is the Flame of Genius, the true deliverer of the Race. He was chained by his father and mother in fear of Urizen's jealousy, but we know that he will break free at last, and bring his living fire into the hearts of the chosen of the peoples.

The book contains but five pages, of which the most beautiful is a design of a boy and girl with arms wound around each other, running over a hill-top, with a passionate sunset sky behind them. The "Book of Los," which must not be confounded with the Song, appeared in the same year. The Print Room has no copy, so we must descend to the Library, which happily possesses one. It consists of four chapters on the[Pg 123] old themes, written in a sort of metrical prose. The frontispiece, representing a woman in the characteristic attitude so often adopted by Blake—the figure being seated on the ground, with head supported on knees in a mysterious lone place among rocks—is an arresting and powerful design. The writing in this book is particularly fine and clear. It is the last of Blake's "London Books of Prophecy."

What shall I say of "Jerusalem, the Emanation of the Giant Albion"—this longest and perhaps most mystical of all Blake's dithyrambic books?

It was written, as well as the "Milton," during the Felpham period, though probably added to, and finally finished after his return to London.

43

Those who have heard the extraordinary tone-poem called "Also sprach Zarathustra," by Richard Strauss, may not think it far-fetched to suggest a parallel between revolutionary, chaotic, yet somehow great music, such as it is, and the so-called poem of "Jerusalem." To the authors of both, the classical, the established forms of expression belonging to their respective arts, seem outworn, inadequate, cramped. They feared to trust the new wine of their fermenting ideas to the old bottles of recognized form, and each has invented for himself a way of escape—somewhat dangerous, nay, almost suicidal—from the pressure of precedent, law, and order. Strange harmonies, horrid discords, sweetness as of honey, to be succeeded by a sharp acridity like that of unripe lemons, great marshalled orchestral forms, and wild abortive sounds, tormenting alike to ear and heart, are to be discerned in "Zarathustra," not without irrational excitement, anger, dismay, and occasional delight on the part of the hearer. And in "Jerusalem" is it not much the same?

With an Olympian audacity Blake writes, "When this Verse was first dictated to me, I considered a[Pg 124] monotonous cadence like that used by Milton and Shakespeare, and all writers of English blank verse, derived from the modern bondage of rhyming, to be a necessary and indispensable part of verse. But I soon found that in the mouth of a true orator, such monotony was not only awkward, but as much a bondage as rhyme itself. I therefore have produced a variety in every line, both of cadences and number of syllables. Every word and every letter is studied and put into its place; the terrific numbers are reserved for the terrific parts, the mild and gentle for the mild and gentle parts, and the prosaic for the inferior parts; all are necessary to each other; Poetry fettered, fetters the human race."

Self-assertion such as this is the apology for arts like those of Strauss and Walt Whitman, and our very admiration for Blake's youthful lyrical gift compels us to lament that his muse was brought at last, after those early days of soaring flight, to wading through such quagmires of so-called poetry as this and the ensuing book. Mysticism had engulfed the poet in its dim cloud, though poetic phrases and passages like crystal dew glitter amid the gloom.

The "Jerusalem" may be regarded as an attempted poetic statement of Blake's mystic philosophy regarding the development of humanity and its various states.

	I	give	you	the	end	of	a	golden	string
Only		wind		it		into		a	ball,
It	will	lead	you	in	at		Heaven's		gate

Built in Jerusalem's wall,

writes Blake in the course of the book. Messrs. Ellis and Yeats have wound it into a very tangible ball, taking the symbolizism of the four Zoas as the clue to the whole mystery. Blake mentions the Zoas here frequently: "Four universes round the mundane egg [Pg 125]remain chaotic" (nothing could be more true!) "One to the North Urthona; one to the South Urizen; one to the East Luvah; one to the west Thamas. They are the four Zoas that stood around the throne divine." But if the symbolism of the Zoas is in reality woven into the very tissue of the story, and forms its vital and coherent argument, it must be discovered on some mathematical principle very foreign, and, indeed, repugnant to the lover of true poetry. It is in no sense obvious or sequential. The value of the book lies, not in its poetical merit, nor even primarily in its mystic significance, but in the insight which it affords into the byways of Blake's mind. The knowledge of his opinions gained here (they have been shortly commented on in a former chapter) enable us to form correct estimates of the scope of his plastic art, and his outlook on the world. Messrs. Maclaggan and Russell have edited a plain-typed and unillustrated edition of "Jerusalem," and promise an expository essay on it to follow in due course, so that to earnest readers its study will be greatly facilitated. The book is concerned with one Albion, the father as it would seem of all created men, and Los (Time) who is his friend. Jerusalem and Vala are his emanations—Jerusalem being his wife. The city of Golgonooza—that is, I believe, Spiritual Art—is also described, and bears its part in the story.

On page 13, line 30, we read, "Around Golgonooza lies the land of death eternal; a land of pain and misery and despair and ever-brooding misery"—the repetition of the word "misery," does not sound as if every word had been studied and put in its place! But the idea that the beautiful city of spiritual Art should be built in the midst of pain and despair reminds one of a similar idea of Goethe's, "Art enshrines the great sadness of the world, but is itself not sad." And the following lines develop the suggestion, page 16, line 61: "All things[Pg 126] acted on Earth are seen in the Bright Sculptures of Los's Halls, and every age renews its powers from these works. With every pathetic story possible to happen from Hate or Wayward Love and every sorrow and distress is carved here."

The introduction of localities, streets and districts, has an almost ludicrous effect, as for instance in the following lines: "What are those golden builders doing near mournful ever-weeping Paddington?" Is it, one wonders, a prophetic announcement of the erection of the Great

Western Terminus? Had Blake possessed the saving grace of humour, he would never have committed such laughter-provoking solecisms as this and other passages of the same kind Humour is a means of restoring and keeping the balances true. It assists the sense of proportion, and like a fresh wind blows the cobwebs away; but, alas! Blake had no faintest trace of it.

In a kind of Dionysiac rage he has flung his noble ideas, original conceptions, pell-mell into the cauldron along with mere windy, mouth-filling rodomontade. There is a great deal of confused noise, but by snatches we distinguish the half-drowned but heavenly music. The fact is that his material (God-dictated, as he thought) so excited him that he was unable to deal with it, unable to direct the heat of his genius into fusing the heterogeneous mass into the perfect artistic unity. The vision unnerved him, and he all but lost his balance. Well might he too have cried:

A veil 'twixt us and Thee, dread Lord,
A veil 'twixt us and Thee,
Lest we should hear too clear, too clear
And unto madness see.

The illustrations to the book have all the concentration, power and grasp which the literary matter lacks. The pages seem to throb beneath the teeming forms[Pg 127] of life with which his hand has adorned them. Each in the disposition of the beautiful writing is a picture. Wild passionate little figures, drawn with exquisite feeling, leap, climb, and fly about some of the borders while on others the writing is interrupted and entwined with creeping tendrils, or adorned with flames, stars, serpents, and processions of insects—a riot of decoration.

"Jerusalem" is a folio of 100 pages, one side of each leaf only being printed. From the first page to the twenty-fifth of the Museum copy the writing is in black, while the designs are left white outlined in black, on a dense sable ground. Pages 26 to 50 are in deep green, the printed designs being sometimes finished by hand, the deepest tones being laid on with a brush full of heavy colour. Pages 51 to 100 are again black and white—the black being always of great intensity.

In the first plate a man is seen entering through a door into darkness, with a lamp in his hand. This is our old friend Los entering into the dark places of Albion's mind—Albion having turned his back on "the Divine Vision." Curiously poetical suggestions are to be found in the title-page, whereon a cherubim with covering wings weeps over a beautiful prostrate female. This lovely body forms the central vein of a rose leaf, and is incorporated in its vegetable life. But above the woman's head are the wings that have become atrophied, and the moon and stars, like the eyes of a peacock's feathers, are seen on them, suggesting reminiscences and possibilities of spiritual development in "Vegetative humanity" beyond verbal expression. Glanced at as a whole without discriminating the parts, this fanciful and Gothic conception bears a strange resemblance to a butterfly. Did not the Greeks find in the butterfly a symbol of the immortality of the soul and its renewal in youth, and Blake, who was so profoundly sensitive to analogies of this kind, was not likely to have created[Pg 128] this obvious resemblance accidentally. Everything is with him significant.

Is it a dryad who lies outstretched on page 23 with the rising sap of her vegetable life stirring within her fibrous extremities, and awakening her to some dim half-painful consciousness. And below her, what hints of strange buried gnomic life, of Titans convulsively heaving like volcanoes in the dark earth, of creatures begotten of rocks and tree-roots, living like the suckers of plants in the fissures and crannies of deep strata!

Again, on page 33 appears the beautiful weird fantasy that I have named a dryad. The sun and the moon shine on her simultaneously, and her rudimentary limbs appear now to be branches and again to be embryonic wings. A sort of vampire bat is poised above her. At the top of the same page a man with the world under his foot like a stool would seem to have been saved fainting in the arms of an effulgent divine Being from some threatening danger.

I pondered long over this design before finding the clue, which I now believe is to be found in these words, on the previous page, in "Jerusalem": "The reasoning spectre stands between man and his immortal imagination."

On Plate 53 is represented a woman sitting enthroned on a sunflower, her double wings form a sort of baldachino above her head. She has a triple tiara from which flames arise in a pyramidal shape, and the sun, the moon, and the stars are contained in her vast wings. The vegetative human has blossomed in the sunflower of spiritual life. No longer "the starry heavens are fled from the mighty limbs of Albion," but instead of separation there is a large union. "In every bosom a universe expands," and "everything exists in the human imagination," are words which help to explain this curious design.

[Pg 129]A coloured print of the same plate, very sumptuous and rich, was exhibited in the Carfax Galleries in January, 1894.

45

A beautiful drawing on page 46 gives the meeting of Vala with Jerusalem and her children, but as an artist's forms often contain more in them than the obvious expression of a fact, so here one may permit oneself to see another meaning underlying this, as the ancient text underlies the palimpsest. Vala may also have an analogy with Death, who like a veiled woman meets a mother with her children. As she lifts her veil, and looks upon one among the group, the child takes flight and attempts to draw his sister after him. Blake, who seldom made his faces characteristic, but was satisfied with making them merely typical, has given this woman's face a piteous expression of fear and entreaty.

A notable plate is that representing the Crucifixion, the motive of which, when disengaged from the confused material of the book, is discovered to be the bed-rock or foundation, the radical thought, at the base of "Jerusalem" and the next work "Milton." Jesus the Saviour is Eternal Imagination slain by men, who nail it to the "stems of generation," that is, kill it through the opacity of the senses and the limitations of sexual life. Just in the same way Orc, the deliverer, who is a type or other aspect of Jesus, is Genius, and by man is nailed on to the rocks of Mount Atlas.

Looking through the pages of "Jerusalem," vague memories of Norse sagas, of dim carved stalls in old Gothic cathedrals, of the cold cellar-like air that sighs through their aisles and chapels, come to one and cause a delightful and yet fearful shudder. But the designs savour only in a fleeting irrational way of these things, having a wholly unique character of their own.

The "Prophetic Books" reproduced by Messrs. Ellis[Pg 130] and Yeats are not taken from the British Museum copies it may be as well to remark here, and the variation in the disposition of the light and shade is great in the various copies, though the outlines are always the same, being printed off the same plate, of course. The finest known copy of "Jerusalem" was sold at Messrs. Sotheby's among other Blake treasures belonging to Lord Crewe for the sum of £83.

"Milton," the last of the published "Books of Prophecy," produced in 1804, is a small quarto of forty-five printed pages, coloured by hand in the old radiant manner. The preface, beautiful but sibylline, is an appeal to all men to worship and exalt Imagination, which in ancient times in the Christ-form, says Blake, "walked upon England's mountains green." "Would to God that all the Lord's people were prophets"—that is "seers"—he quotes with profound earnestness at the end.

The "poem" itself opens more intelligibly than most of the later books with a mythic story concerning one Palamabron and the horses of the plough; of Satan, who persuaded him to be allowed to drive the horses for one day, and of the dire confusion, strife, and tragedy resulting from Palamabron's consent.

The story bears a distant analogy to the Phaethon myth, for Palamabron represents, according to Messrs. Ellis and Yeats, the "imaginative impulse," while Satan is the dark angel who erects the barriers of reason limited by moral laws and senses around humanity. It was impossible for one to do the work of the other.

The definite incidents with which "Milton" so hopefully opens are soon lost sight of, and the loosely-fitted framework, ill-adjusted and weak, contains a tangled woof of mysticism, from which the end of the thread is so difficult of extraction, that I for one must plead that the trouble of "winding a golden ball" seems hardly[Pg 131] worth while, though it is no doubt possible and profitable to the student of mysticism. Milton's part in the book is perhaps the hardest to decipher. But we find him undertaking a journey from heaven, through earth and hell. "Milton" seems specially dear to Blake because he made Satan the supreme study of his greatest poem. Blake, as we know, had very original thoughts concerning Satan, and regarded him as the world's angel of light, a most respectable person indeed, for he is the enforcer of the moral law as evolved by divided generative humanity.

Milton like Blake recognized this highly respectable aspect of Satan, whereas the world, says our poet in "The Everlasting Gospel," frequently mistakes Satan for Christ:

The   vision   of   Christ   that   thou   dost   see,
Is my vision's greatest enemy,

and it creates an abortive kind of hell-bat to take the *rôle* of Satan,—a very confused state of affairs, which leads to no little deception and opacity in men's minds. The old themes of free-love for the sake of the spirit, and the denunciation of "Nature's cruel holiness," occupy much of the book, in which the mythic personages, Leutha, Rintrah, Ololon, and Enitharmon move up and down in dream-like procession. The ease with which these shadowy beings enter each other's personalities, divide, and separate again into manifold emanations and spectres, suggest the multitudinous globes into which a drop of quicksilver may be divided, uniting again on contact into several large ones, and finally forming the unit from which they were first divided. Fascinating as is the experiment with mercury, it becomes confusing and even tiresome when the appearing and vanishing parties are persons with names and presumably characters.

[Pg 132]One passage full of the old poetical loveliness of which Blake had been past master must be quoted. It shows that the beauty of nature at Felpham, with its distracting fascination, entered the soul of the poet, despite all theories and philosophizings.

Thou hearest the nightingale begin the Song of Spring:
The lark sitting upon his earthy bed: just as the morn
Appears; listens silent: then springing from the waving cornfield, loud
He leads the choir of Day! trill, trill, trill, trill,
Mounting upon the wings of light into the great expanse:
Re-echoing against the lovely blue and shining shell.
His little throat labours with inspiration, every feather,
On throat and breast and wings vibrates with the effluence divine,
All Nature listens silent to him, and the awful sun
Stands still upon the mountains looking on this little bird,
With eyes of soft humility, and wonder, love and awe.
Then loud from their green covert all the birds begin their song.
The thrush, the linnet and the goldfinch, robin and the wren,
Awake the Sun from his sweet reverie upon the mountains.
The nightingale again assays his song and through the day
And through the night warbles luxuriant: every bird of song
Attending his loud harmony with admiration and love.

To this passage succeeds another of like beauty, a Flora's Feast of colour and scent.

Thou perceivest the flowers put forth their precious odours:
And none can tell how from so small a centre comes such sweet,
Forgetting that within that centre Eternity expands
Its ever-during doors, that Og and Anak fiercely guard.
First ere the morning breaks, joy opens in the flowery bosoms,
Joy even to tears, which the Sun rising dries: first the wild thyme
And meadowsweet downy and soft, waving among the reeds,
Light springing in the air, lead the sweet dance: they wake
The honeysuckle sleeping on the oak: the flaunting beauty
Revels along the wind: the white-thorn, lovely may
Opens her many lovely eyes: listening, the rose still sleeps,
None dare to wake her: soon she bursts her crimson-curtained bed
And comes forth in the majesty of beauty; every flower,
The pink, the jessamine, the wall-flower, the carnation,
The jonquil, the mild lily opes her heavens: every tree
And herb and flower soon fill the ear with an innumerable dance,
Yet all in order sweet and lovely. Men are sick with love.

[Pg 133]Oh! how gladly the ear and heart rest on passages such as these, after toiling through the arid wilds of non-poetical occultism!

As usual the illustrations are turned to with keen delight. The iridescent pages recall the charms of the "Songs of Innocence and Experience." Take it all in all the colour in this last prophetic book combines a clarity and brilliance of tone inferior to no other of Blake's. All is careful, clear and precise, and there are no passages of heavy colouring or impasto work.

Forms, elemental, electric, indicative of unknown forces and conditions of consciousness start from the pages. As in "Jerusalem," every page of writing is adorned, but the colour adds the necessary charm to the forceful designs. Plate 15 represents a muscular male—Michael Angelesque in its modelling—leaping upon a rock and seizing by the shoulders a languid old man. The young man is Milton, starting on his journey "to annihilate the selfhood of deceit and false forgiveness." The old man is Albion seated on the Rock of Ages, his legs immersed in the sea of Time and Space, his nerveless arms supported on the tables of the Law. Above them both, on a semi-circular plane of light, the Eternals are seen, passing in procession in a kind of ecstatic choric dance. Three play on instruments of music, while two others toss balls of light in joyous abandon. The rhythmic character of these dancers, their robes fetched out like clouds upon the wind, and the colour translucent and vivid as that of a border of April flowers, makes one think of the fair works with which Luca della Robbia has set the dark old streets of Florence, of which, as some one has poetically said, they would seem to be the "wall-flowers."

The two other specially noteworthy plates are full-page designs, entitled respectively William and Robert. It is evident that they are the spiritual likenesses of[Pg 134] Blake and that younger brother with whom he always maintained such close communion. A burning star emitting fountains of light falls beside each brother, while their bodies thrown backwards, and their faces skywards, seem to indicate the abandon of themselves to spiritual influences. The senses are not the limits put upon their perceptions. The Infinite spirit, the "Poetic Genius," thrills through their entire beings as the sunshine through a dewdrop.

Let not the profane smile when they learn that the star is in reality Milton! For it is written, "so Milton's shadow fell Precipitant loud thundering into the sea of Time and Space."

Then   first   I   saw   him   in   the   zenith   as   a   falling   star, Descending   perpendicular,   swift   as   the   swallow   or   swift, And on my left foot falling on the tarsus, enter'd there.

So there can be no doubt as to what the star symbolizes in the design. The articulation, the tense nervous drawing of these two figures is remarkable, even for Blake, and the light throbbing with rainbow hues, and the intense darkness, against which it is contrasted, are boldly handled, while the weird colouring of the dead Robert, whose skin has the tone and lustre of gun metal, conduce to make these two designs of great imaginative appeal. Space has only allowed me to call attention to the most remarkable of the plates in this and the other "Prophetic Books," but enough has been said to indicate the extraordinary range of their expression.

To see Blake's work of this kind is to enjoy a new experience. Many of the pictorial representations we have reviewed seem to be disregardful of Nature, if one dare say it, *above* Nature altogether! Yet so clearly are they discriminated, so minutely are the parts made out, that we are compelled to realize that they are[Pg 135] copied from visions definitely seen by Blake's inner eye, and energetically seized upon by him. And it is this quality in them which so powerfully acts on the spectator, assuring him that indeed "More things exist in heaven and earth than our philosophy dreams of." But besides these tremendous imaginative creations, there occur touching and beautiful transcripts from Nature, low-lying hills, under a great sky, waving field grasses and delicate spiders' webs accurately observed and represented, as far as they go, proving that Dame Nature was not so utterly repudiated by Blake but that at times he saw and loved her for her own sake, in spite of all his theories.

Still, the great word for him—the only word fit to bear the burden of his tremendous thoughts—was always, as with Michael Angelo, the human form, which, in its varieties of type and action, seemed to him alone suited to express his deep meanings and spiritual ideas. As for the prophecies themselves, they can never be largely read, nor in any sense popular, though, to use Mr. W. M. Rossetti's words, "a reader susceptible to poetic influence cannot make light of them; nor can one who has perused Mr. Swinburne's essay" (or, we may add, Messrs. Ellis and Yeats' work) "affect to consider that they lack meaning—positive and important, though not definite and developed meaning." So now we take leave of these mystic books of revelation, which, whatever our personal estimate of them may be, stand alone in literature for intrinsic and unique qualities.

[Pg 136]

CHAPTER X
WORK IN ILLUSTRATION

Blake's work in illustration is considered by many persons to be finer than the embodiment of his original conceptions in art.

There is perhaps something to be said for this point of view. In the designs to the "Prophetic Books" his over-heated brain attempted the production in visible images of conceptions not matured—hints, scraps, vague but immense suggestions. His unfettered imagination set sail on a shoreless ocean of speculative thinking, and kept to no recognized course, made for no definite port. Roaming hither and thither on the wide dim sea of his ever-shifting thoughts, we sometimes long to see his imagination at work in a more limited, a more definite area.

And so when other minds circumscribed this area, giving him a central pole around which to group his ideas, we find no loss of individuality, no pale reflection of another's conceptions, but a passionate concentration of original thinking on the subject prescribed, resulting in the development of an unsuspected point of view, a new aspect.

I am not speaking of illustrations such as those he executed as mere task-work to gain a living, like the engravings to Mary Wollstonecraft's Stories, or those for Hayley's Ballads. For these subjects had not enough matter, depth or scope to attract his thoughts or engage his sympathies. As illustrator to Dante, Milton, [Pg 137]Shakespeare, Virgil and the Book of Job, Blake worked with all his best and most characteristic powers under his command, and the more effective, vital and original for being concentrated.

In the same year in which he produced the last of the "London Books of Prophecy," 1795, we find him illustrating a so-called translation of Bürger's "Lenore." In spite of the weakness and wilful inaccuracy of the English version, Blake seized with power on the spirit of the Teutonic legend, and gave the edition, a copy of which is in the Print Room (a quarto), three fine designs, of which the first is the most forceful.

We cannot linger over the designs which Hayley commissioned Blake to execute for his "Ballads on Animals." From the engraver's point of view they are specially fine, as the execution is very delicate, and reaches a state of high finish seldom attempted by Blake. Perhaps he wished to atone for paucity of inspiration by elaborate labour. Certain it is that he worked in bonds and trammels. The subjects were not interesting to him. Hayley might well say, in his lumberingly playful way, that "our good Blake was in labour with a young lion," when he was engaged on the plate representing that animal. The labour was immense, for the conception had no vitality. Blake scourged his imagination into a degree of liveliness sufficient to make "the Horse" and "the Eagle" arresting and uncommon work, but the shackles were on his hands, because on his spirit, and he knew it.

Young's "Night Thoughts," which we take up next, bears the date 1797. Blake made no less than five hundred and thirty-seven water-colour drawings for this poem, but only forty-three designs were eventually selected for publication, and these were reproduced as uncoloured engravings. Till a short while ago, Mr. Bain of the Haymarket possessed the whole series of [Pg 138]water-colour drawings, but they have now passed by purchase into the hands of an American collector. Through the kindness of Mr. Frederic Shields, who many years ago made tracings and copies from the unpublished designs, I am enabled to give reproductions of some of the most striking, though of course not in colour. (It will be remembered that Mr. Shields wrote the very powerful chapter on Young's "Night Thoughts" which is included in the second volume of Gilchrist's Life.) The designs published with the poem are larger than those we are accustomed to see in Blake's books, and the disposition of them on the pages, of which the middle is occupied by the printed type enclosed in rectangular spaces, is not effective. We miss our artist's beautiful fluent writing, and the type produces a bald staring impression on the beholder. When, too, the head and shoulders of a figure appear above the placard and the feet and legs below, as in one or two plates, we are irresistibly reminded of sandwich men. The want of colour also is a crying need in these large, pale, somewhat flat plates. The engravings are executed with great lightness, though with a certain monotony of line. They are slightly shaded, and have a distinguishing quality of purity and breadth. What luminous conceptions and stimulating fancies they contain! though it must also be admitted that there are a few plates which seem unworthy of Blake, being diffuse, tame, uninspired.

Plate 16 represents the "Aspiration of the Soul for Immortality" in a beautiful symbolic female figure holding a lyre and fluttering upward, but confined to the earth by chains around the ankles.

Plates 25 and 26 are, perhaps, the most tremendous in the book. In one Time creeps towards the spectator, while in the other he half-leaps, half-flies in his headlong course away.

[Pg 139]As one turns the pages one is fain to exclaim of the artist that he breathed the fine thin air of the mountain tops, that indeed he lived "in the high places of thought."

I have an impression that Blake drew much of his inspiration from watching the ever-changing cloud forms of the sky. We know that his designs gained actually very little from the beautiful natural scenery of Felpham, that indeed Nature seemed to close round him like a wall. "Natural objects always did and do weaken, deaden, and obliterate imagination in me," he wrote in his MS. notes to Wordsworth. Strange words to come from a painter-poet. A top room in London with a good view of the sky were all the conditions which he found necessary for the expression of his genius. In the vastness of the heavens, clear and deeply blue, or peopled with glistening clouds, or set with large peaceful stars, which spread themselves before his upward gaze, Blake found that impetus to creation which most genius finds in nature or humanity.

He had set himself the task of probing the world of appearances, and revealing the world of spiritual causes. To say that he succeeded in representing this pictorially would be to assert that an impossibility had been achieved, but he got nearer to the goal than any other artist before or since, not even excepting D. G. Rossetti and G. F. Watts, whose affinity with Blake's genius is as close as their manifestation of it is different.

The better to realize his aim Blake stripped his drawing of everything that was not essential to the idea he wished to represent. There is never a single redundant accessory. He never stayed his upward or outward flight to represent a lovely landscape, woman's dainty dress, flashing jewels, bloomy fruit. Typical or merely suggested natural scenes under a great sky are the usual settings of the human forms who were to him,[Pg 140] as to his master Michael Angelo, the only language coherent enough to express the innerness and the infinity of spirit.

He seldom chose to inclose his figures in interiors, and such drawings as he has left of places from which the sky cannot be seen are so rare as to startle when we come across them. It may be that from Blake Walt Whitman learned to say, "I swear I will never mention love or death inside a house."

The sea fascinated his imagination, and he has left characteristic records of it. But for the most part that which he saw with his "corporeal eye" appeared to him as merely the type of what was unseen. He climbed along the jutting peninsula of sense to its farthest point, where, giddy with the immensity of the unsuspected forces revealed to him, he clung, neither angel nor mortal, but partaking to a certain degree of the conditions of both. When in this mystic condition of consciousness he focussed his mind on the "Night Thoughts," the pencilled ideas resulting are liberal, spacious, empyrean.

But Blake's most forcible and poetical thinking on the subject of Death is crystallized in the delicately gleaming drawings for Blair's "Grave."

True, the drawings are not reproduced in Cromek's edition of the poem as they left Blake's hand. The story of Cromek's mean transaction has already been retold in these pages. Schiavonetti's plates, beautiful and fluent in execution as they are, have lost that peculiar rugged character, that almost galvanic energy which stamp the original drawings with Blake's hallmark. It must be borne in mind that engraving may alter original drawings much in the same way as does the transposition of a musical phrase from the original into a foreign key. The melody is the same, but the mood of it is different. It becomes dull instead of[Pg 141] bright, or plaintive instead of triumphant. Schiavonetti's transposing of Blake has made the designs more sweet and less strong, or perhaps less vehement. It is Blake in a new aspect, one so obviously beautiful that all the world admits its loveliness. It is Blake arranged for the many, not Blake for the intimate few!

The stanzas he wrote in dedication to Queen Charlotte form such a fitting introduction to the plates that we quote them:

The door of death is made of gold
That mortal eyes cannot behold,
But when the mortal eyes are closed
And cold and pale the limbs reposed,
The soul awakes and wond'ring sees
In her mild hands the golden keys.
The grave is heaven's golden gate,
And rich and poor around it wait.
O Shepherdess of England's fold,
Behold this gate of pearl and gold.

To dedicate to England's Queen
The visions that my soul has seen,
And, by her kind permission bring,
What I have borne on solemn wing,
From the vast regions of the grave;
Before her throne my wings I wave,
Bowing before my sov'reign's feet.
The grave produced these blossoms sweet,
In mild repose from earthly strife;
The blossoms of eternal life.

And now Blake comes to close quarters with the subject that had haunted him all his life, the dark web on which he had woven so many bright, half-defined fancies.

Again we discern a *point d'appui* between him and Michael Angelo. The thoughts of neither of them were long away from death. Michael Angelo wrestled with the dark angel and brought away from the encounter the profound and intimate thoughts that he has[Pg 142] enshrined in the Medici Tombs of San Lorenzo. Never has the human soul—save perhaps Beethoven's—apprehended more closely the mystery, the terror, the mingled shrinking and awe of the grave, yet at the same time its hope, than he did in the Sacristy of the Medici Chapel. And in all plastic art, the only things to which these fateful sculptures may be likened in their qualities of rapt and sincere thinking, united to imagination and insight, are the designs, which Blake made to illustrate Blair's "Grave."

The great Florentine, it is true, wrought colossally in enduring marble before all the world, while the obscure Blake, two centuries later, traced out his thoughts on paper, his designs being known to comparatively few persons; but the conceptions of the two brains are allied, and the works of the two hands are own brothers.

Blair's conventional and smooth verses in Blake's case have nothing to do with the matter. They merely form the pegs on which he cast the great garment of his thoughts. Death—the Grave!—his intense and fervent spirit so brooded on the subject that the result is no mere illustration of Blair's text, but invention. The poem in his handling has enlarged itself out of all knowledge, and turned to us an unfamiliar face, new and enriching conceptions. Blair merely indicated the track on which his pioneer spirit journeyed heedfully and musingly, through the dim country of Death. Piercing all accepted theology, he would fain seize the very heart of the elusive mystery. "What *is* Death?" he asks; "let me peer into the grave unshrinkingly and see for myself." And from the grave he brings this triumphant answer, "Death is Life, this Life only is Death; you have but to die to conquer Death"; or in Walt Whitman's prosaic but arresting phrase, "To die is different from what anyone supposes, and luckier."

[Pg 143]We reproduce the most significant of the plates.

In "The Soul exploring the Recesses of the Grave," we see a shuddering yet resolved man determinately bringing himself to the close contemplation of death. He remains above the vault on the hillside trying to pierce the moonlit earth with his limited human vision; but his imagination, his soul, penetrates where he cannot enter—yet!

In the likeness of a fair woman with a lamp, like the Greek Psyche, she tiptoes delicately into the arched hollow beneath the hill, and gazes alarmed but steadfast on a dead body wrapped in flickering flames. It is to be noted that the man whose soul regards death so closely is already on the mountain tops, he has "lifted up his eyes unto the hills," and his figure set against the sky has an indefinable air of separateness from ordinary humanity.

The plate entitled "The Soul hovering over the Body reluctantly parting with Life" satisfies with a strange and unearthly delight. No Diana ever hung more yearningly above her Endymion than this beautiful and tender soul lingers, in loving reluctance to part, above the stiff human tenement she has just quitted. Presently she will take her darting flight through the window and over the mountains and up into the illimitable glory of the distant sunrise. There is the hush and the blessedness of a great silence on this dim silver dawn, suggesting the spiritual correspondence between it and the dawning life of the newly-released soul. Was it a recollection of that younger brother, Robert, so dearly loved, that taught Blake the pathetic dignity of the composed limbs, the sculptured calm of the dead face?

The "Death of the Strong Wicked Man" is a savage contrast to the peace, the musical pause, of the last-mentioned design.

[Pg 144]In "Milton," Blake writes:

Judge   then   of   thyself;   thy   Eternal   Lineaments   explore, What is eternal and what changeable, and what annihilable.

And he answers the question in the forms given to these passing souls, some being closely analogous to their mortal appearances, others changing even to sex, while others again have passed from age into a state of perpetual youth.

This latter is the case in the plate called "Death's Door." "Age on crutches is hurried by a tempest into the open door of the Grave, while above sits a young man—'the renovated man in light and glory'—his beautiful young head thrown up to the sky, his mouth full of inspired song, his whole virile body expressing ideal beauty, rapture, glad new life."

No one but Michael Angelo could have drawn with strong felicitous hand the glorious youth atop of the grave as Blake has done. The whole allegory is so intellectually definite, so succinctly expressed that thought and its body form are here identical. But the strangest flower of his thoughts on the grave, blossoms in the picture called "The Re-Union of the Soul and the Body." Descending like a bolt from the blue, cleaving the smoke ascending from the fires of consuming materialism, the soul embraces with passionate joy the strong male body, which struggles from the grave to enfold her. Cleansing and fusing fires flame around them. The beauty of the drawing—the melodious curves of the downward plunging "soul," the delicious foreshortening of the leg, the swirl of the white drapery—has stricken into poetic lines the forcefulness of flight, the passion of re-union. This emotional conception moves the heart strangely. It is the promise of St. Paul here visibly consummated, that a spiritual body shall at last clothe the shivering unhoused soul.

[Pg 145]"States change," Blake wrote, "but Individual Identities never change nor cease." And now take last of all, but not least, the plate called the "Day of Judgment." Nothing daunted by the long array of "Last Judgments" that have been executed from Orcagna to Michael Angelo, Blake must needs give *his* rendering of the subject; and an original one it is, though he can hardly avoid—even *he*!—the traditional disposition of the main parts of the picture.

51

But what freshness, what new life and new motives he has introduced into this subject, hoary with extreme age. The spirits ascending into Paradise are as lovely as heart and eye of man could wish. Orcagna's conception of the beatified souls in Santa Maria, whose profiles Ruskin likened to "lilies laid together in a garden border," is not more delightful in its artless way than is Blake's. The children of wrath, snake-encircled, howling, and falling head foremost into the abyss, recall the terrors, the uncouth and wild imagination of "Urizen" and one of the plates in "America." But here Schiavonetti's graceful and civilizing hand has passed over each figure, and he has contrived in some indefinable way to smooth away the too austere and savage strength of this latest born of the "*Dies illa*" of art.

I have not mentioned the first plate, which represents Christ with the Keys of the Grave in his hand, because my function is chiefly that of praise. But I ought perhaps to point out, what is however painfully obvious, that Blake always failed in any attempt to represent Jesus. Whether he was hampered to a degree beyond his strength of liberation by the traditional likeness, the type ascribed to the Saviour, and so could not work in freedom, it is impossible to say authoritatively. But this traditional face of Christ, ploughed as it is into the heart and memory of humanity, probably arose and[Pg 146] disturbed his own soul's independent vision whenever he tried to fix his imagination on the ideal lineaments.

If this were the case, then indeed it is proved beyond question that Blake's work is almost valueless when it is not dependent on his own naked perceptions, his inward recognition of facts, disregardful of all outward corroboration.

Blake's next work in illustration was done for Dr. Thornton, who projected an English edition of Virgil's "Pastorals" for the use of schools, with Ambrose Philips' imitation of Virgil's first eclogue. They were the first and the only woodcuts Blake ever did, and though they bear traces of an unpractised hand, "he put to proof art alien to the artists," and showed his essential mastery of this means of expression in a manner which more than reconciles one to his slight defects of method.

Gilchrist is of opinion that the original designs were a little marred—lost somewhat in expression and drawing in transference to the wood; but Mr. Laurence Binyon, who has lately studied them closely, and has reproduced them with admirable truth, holds a different opinion. He writes, "Blake's conceptions in these illustrations did not take their final form in the drawings; they were only fully realized on the block itself. Hence they have the character of visions called up as if by moonlight out of the darkened surface of the wood, and seem to have no existence apart from it."

They instance the power Blake had in a remarkable degree of concentrating in a few types the essence of his subject. In these blocks it is pastoral life—flocks feeding in lonely stretches of country, the still peace of hills, the might of tempest—that he concentrates and expresses by the roughly executed but exquisitely felt little scenes which are the consummation of his insight into the large natural life of the earth.

[Pg 147]Blake did in these woodcuts, what he could never have achieved, had he sought to do so, in any other of the branches of art practised by him,—namely, he gave truthful because extremely simple impressions of Nature as she appears in her rarer moods. Master as he was of linear design, he was too neglectful of tonic values to interpret with any delicacy the effects of landscape in water-colour or engraving. But here, the very nature and limitations of woodcutting, its necessary economy of means, enabled him for once to express effectively and adequately his great simple generalized impressions.

These pregnant suggestions of his induce a mood sympathetic with the deeper and subtler chords of pantheism.

In one of the most beautiful, but at the same time one of the simplest of the blocks, all the witchery and solemn charm of a remote pastoral neighbourhood is represented in a few typical rural images.

A solitary traveller journeys along a road winding deep between hills, in the last beams of the setting sun. Blake has endowed this darkened landscape with I know not what suggestions of watchful intentness. The wayfarer in some mysterious manner is in its power!

Hands   unseen
Are hanging the night around him fast.
    And again:

The   place   is   silent   and   aware,
It   has   had   its   scenes,   its   joy   and   crimes,
But that is its own affair.

These words of Browning's are singularly apt to express the delicate and profound hints in this little woodcut. The wonderful thing is that Blake *could convey* so much on a slip of paper about three inches by one and a half in size.

[Pg 148]In all the plates we find this strange accent laid on Nature, her awareness, her sombre fateful moods, her listening, and the long patience of her endless waiting. The oft-repeated motive of the shepherding of flocks is treated in no glib or merely idyllic manner, but has the sort of holy peace that befits that most ancient and most gentle of all the occupations of men.

An appreciative critic has said anent these woodcuts, that they prove conclusively that "amid all drawbacks there exists a power in the work of the man of genius which no one but himself can utter fully."

The truth of this remark must be felt by all Blake's admirers with double force and poignancy when they think regretfully of Blair's "Grave," wherein the designs, being engraved by another hand than the father of them, have lost some indefinable note of character belonging to Blake's personality.

And now we come to the greatest series of engravings on a religious subject that have appeared since Albrecht Dürer. The inventions to "Job" are the crown of glorious achievement on the strenuous and austere life of the artist-poet, and of all his work there is nothing so perfect in the dramatic development of the subject, the broad, forceful yet delicate execution, and the poetic sensibility which animates the entire series.

It appears that Blake's lifelong friend, Mr. Butts, bought from him a series of twenty-one water-colour drawings or "Inventions" from the Book of Job.

(This set of drawings, be it remarked, together with twenty-two brilliant proof impressions on India paper of the engravings afterwards made from them, were sold to Mr. Quaritch on March 31st, 1903, at the sale of the Crewe collection of Blake's works, for the sum of £5,600.)

I have seen one water-colour (presumably not one of[Pg 149] the original set done for Thomas Butts, though probably a repliqua) of Satan pouring a vial containing the plague of boils on the prostrate body of Job. It is interesting to compare it with the final form the design assumed in the engraving (Plate 6 in the Book of Job) done for John Linnell. Owing to the courtesy of Sir Charles Dilke, to whom the picture now belongs, we have been enabled to reproduce it. It will at once be seen that, in the engraving the management of the light is more satisfactory, because it is comprehensible, than in the water-colour; while the cloud-forms are less conventional and rounder. The bat-like wings with which Satan is furnished in the painting have been sacrificed in the engraving. Job's wife has been put into tone, whereas in the water-colour, the visible side of her, which ought to have been in dense shadow, was in full light. The whole design has been pulled together, gaining an impressiveness and unity altogether wanting in the earlier work. Blake's passion for "determinate outline" (irrespective of its appearance in Nature), and contempt for truth of tone in colour, gives the water-colour a mapped-out definitive appearance in its background of scenery,—despite the magnificent qualities of imagination and draughtsmanship displayed in the treatment of the figures,—which somehow recalls the work of such masters as Paolo Uccello.

Mr. Linnell, deeply impressed with the lofty and imaginative character of the water-colours done for Mr. Butts, commissioned a complete set of engravings to be executed from them by Blake's hand, for which he paid £150 in instalments of £2 to £3 weekly—the largest sum Blake had ever received for any one series.

On glancing through them it will at once be noticed that his style of engraving had undergone a change during the last period of his life.

[Pg 150]"The Canterbury Pilgrimage," which he had executed fifteen years previously, exhibited the old hard and dry manner of engraving which he had adopted from Basire in its most accentuated form. (For the convenience of classification I have included that picture among the loose drawings, engravings, and water-colours for consideration in a later chapter, but it would be well for the student to look at it now, the better to appreciate the freedom, grace and power of the engravings in the "Job" series.)

On one of the many pleasant days Blake spent with Linnell at North End, Hampstead, the latter showed him some choice engravings of Marc Antonio and his pupil Bononsoni, and from this latter's work Blake suddenly apprehended the possibilities, the scope, that lay for him in the engraver's art. In the school of Basire much of the work was accomplished by a laborious and indiscriminate process of cross-hatching.

It is true that Blake by the sheer force of his genius had made this style answer in a manner to his needs of expression, but it was work performed in an unnecessarily confined technique.

53

When he came to study the Italian school of engraving he found to his delight that every stroke was made to tell. Nothing blotchy or muddled, no careless cross-hatching, no "lozenges or dots" were admitted, and Blake quickly appreciated the wider range of effects obtainable by this Italian manner, and engrafted its main principles on to his own characteristic style. Of that characteristic style, as we know, the beauty of outline, the care for its preservation whenever possible, was the main principle. And here in the school of Marc Antonio and Bononsoni he found that principle adopted as the basis of beauty in engraving, every other consideration being made subservient to it. The conflict and want of unity of effect, resultant on making [Pg 151]compromises with other principles of art,—such as subtlety of modelling, delicate distinctions in values, imitation of textures, intricacy of detail,—had not disturbed the dignity of the Italian school, which consciously sacrificed variety and a wide range of effects in order to keep the work of the burin as broad and simple as possible, the outline always being insisted on as the chief subject of alterations, while the shading and modelling were comprehensively indicated by long curved lines, close together, only crossing and intersecting in the darkest parts. The beauty and freedom of the "Job" engravings are a revelation of the final grace and power achieved by Blake through his appreciation of the legitimate functions of an art pre-eminently concerned with line.

The Book of Job is one of the world's great epics. It voices man's need of belief in God; it is the cry of one pierced to death with the arrows of misfortune, yet asserting with passionate faith, "Though He slay me, yet will I trust in Him." Earthquake, famine, bereavements, pestilence cannot eradicate from man the deep-rooted assurance that God not only exists, but is just and loving, and the Book of Job is the supreme poetical expression of this fundamental belief.

As such, it welded itself into Blake's imagination, and the designs he made to illustrate it are worthy in all respects to be set alongside the ancient tragic text.

Plate 1 represents Job, his wife, and their sons and daughter kneeling around them, praising God at the rising of the sun. Their flocks and herds surround them, and a noble tree—on which their musical instruments are hung—overshadows them; in the background, at the base of rocky hills, a Gothic cathedral is daringly set, to typify the soul of worship made visible. "Thus did Job continually." The border that[Pg 152] surrounds the finely-wrought plate is very slight but decorative and thoughtful. An altar with a flaming sacrifice upon it is indicated, with these words inscribed upon its front:

The		letter		killeth,
The	Spirit		giveth	Life,

It is spiritually discerned.

While, above, the words,

Our	Father	which	art	in	Heaven,

Hallowed be Thy name,

set the keynote to the whole work.

Plate 2 contains no less than twenty-three figures, and two scenes are being enacted simultaneously.

Job and his wife still sit beneath the tree with their children, but above them we see the heavens open and God giving power to Satan, who strides like Urizen through flame, to test the uprightness of His servant Job. "This was the day when the sons of God came to present themselves before the Lord, and Satan came also among them to present himself before God." The border is exquisite, light as gossamer, and containing in its fine web-like lines beautiful suggestions. Angels with heads bent beneath Gothic tracery receive the flame and smoke that are the thought-sacrifices of two shepherds, who mind the sleeping flocks in their fold. The next two plates are (3) the Destruction of the Children of Job, and (4) the reception of the news by Job and his wife.

Plate 5 is one of the finest of the series. Job and his wife, sitting on the ruins of their home, give of their straitened means to the blind and halt, while "the angels of their love and resignation," as Gilchrist sympathetically terms them, hallow and beautify the scene. But above, the Almighty sits enthroned, with an expression almost remorseful, and the angels shrink[Pg 153] away in horror, for He has given Satan leave to try Job to the uttermost, only reserving his life. "Behold he is in thy hand, but save his life." Satan, with face averted from the sublime spectacle of Job in his affliction, has concentrated the fires of God into a phial which he is about to pour on his head.

The border is symbolically woven with writhing snakes and thorn-set brambles, among which quick darting flames find their way upwards.

And then follow Plates 6, 7, 8, the workings of the Evil One, the coming of the three friends to Job, and Job raising himself in agony and uttering the frantic words, "Lo, let the night be solitary and let no joyful voice come therein, let the day perish wherein I was born." This suggests "thoughts beyond the reaches of the soul." Then follows the Vision of Eliphaz—very terrible and grand—and Plate 10, "The Just Upright Man is laughed to scorn," in which Job's attitude, the dignity of his grief and faith, are magnificent. "Though He slay me, yet will I trust in Him," is expressed in every line of the noble, piteous figure.

Plate 11—"With Dreams upon my bed thou scarest me and affrightest me with Visions"—has something mediaeval in the grotesqueness and ingeniousness of the horrors depicted. Orcagna's devils, Dürer's "Death and Satan" are not more terrible than Job's tormentors. The words engraved in the border contain all the condensed pain of the race of man, as well as the faith which alone makes it possible to be endured.

And then to all this "storm and stress" succeeds Plate 12, with its suggestions of returning peace and the everlasting calm of the stars. "Lo, all these things worketh God oftentimes with Man to bring back his Soul from the pit to be enlightened with the light of the living!" says the inspired young man to Job, who with the seal of a great suffering set on his face—but a suffering[Pg 154] of which the bitterness is past—sits listening intently as one who suddenly receives light in his soul. The sonorous penetrating words fall on the senses like the music of rain-drops on a thirsty land, and the design grows out of them like a true organic form of which the shape is innate. Oh! the peace of that night sky, and the gentle radiance of the stars set in its depth!

The border is here specially beautiful. "Look upon the heavens, and behold the clouds which are higher than thou"—words that found a responsive echo in the heart of Blake—is the verse inscribed on the robe of a sleeping old man. The border is quick with winged thoughts, floating upwards from his head, in the shape of small men and women, linked in a sinuous succession, which finally reaches a sky, also set with stars, whose clouds have verses written upon them that contribute to a full understanding of Job.

Plate 13, "Then the Lord answered Job out of the whirlwind," continues the gracious and softening influences of the last design. Job and his wife, with tremulous eager hope, look up into the mild face of God, who, clothed and enwreathed by a whirlwind of which Blake only could have suggested the marvellous vortex, stretches His arms in blessing above them. The three friends are prostrated and overwhelmed beneath the force of the blast that encloses God.

And now we come to Plate 14, than which nothing can be imagined more beautiful. "When the morning stars sang together and all the sons of God shouted for joy," are the words beneath and around the border; the six days of creation are indicated in six delicate medallions, which *may* in their turn have suggested the noble series of paintings, of ample scope and poetic imagining, which Sir Edward Burne-Jones executed.

But the main design—God, the centre of the universe, from whom issues Day and Night, the listening rapt[Pg 155] group of Job, his wife, and the comforters, and, above all, the glorious rejoicing ranks of angels—is beautiful almost beyond expression. It is noticeable that on either side appears the arm alone of an angel outside the picture, thus cleverly suggesting the idea of an infinity of this heavenly host. Mrs. Jamieson, in her "Christian Art," says, "The most original and, in truth, the only new and original version of the scripture idea of angels which I have met with is that of William Blake, a poet-painter, somewhat mad as we are told, if indeed his madness were not rather 'the telescope of truth,' a sort of poetical clairvoyance, bringing the unearthly nearer to him than others.

"His adoring angels float rather than fly, and with their half-liquid draperies seem about to dissolve into light and love; and his rejoicing angels—behold them!—sending up their voices with the morning stars, that 'singing in their glory move!'"

The picture has the thrill, the immensity of music in it, and I never look at it without recalling the motive of the last movement of the Choral Symphony.

It resolves all the human suffering, all the incoherent and striving emotions, all the diverse and multiform forces of the Book of Job, into a final harmony and triumph of beauty.

In much the same way the last motive of Beethoven's "Ninth Symphony" rings forth after the tentative, subtle and passionate music of the preceding movements like a shout of joy, the cry of a faith which says—not,[Pg 156] "I have heard, I have learnt, I believe," but, "I *know!* absolutely and for ever!"

Plate 15 shows God pointing out the works that His hand has fashioned. "Behemoth" and Leviathan, in a circular design very Gothic in character, appear below. And to this succeeds Plate 16, "Satan Falling."

Plate 17, in which God appears blessing Job and his wife, while the false comforters hide their diminished heads with an almost comic fright, is distinguished by another of those fine effects of light for which Blake had so great an aptitude. The sun, which forms the nimbus of God's head, emits strange prismatic rays, very beautiful and weird. "Also the Lord accepted Job" shows us Job with his wife and friends offering a fire on an altar before a great sun, which, like God's halo in the previous picture, flashes the same strange light. The design is calm and solemn, and has an exquisite decorative feeling. Immediately below the altar, on some steps which form part of the border, Blake has touchingly and humbly laid his own palette and brushes, as if to indicate that, like Job, his work had been offered and accepted by the Lord.

In Plate 19 Job and his wife are seated beneath a fig-tree in a field of standing corn, gratefully receiving offerings from a father and mother and their two beautiful daughters. "Everyone also gave him a piece of money." The border contains, as usual, amid its palm leaves and angelic figures, verses relating to and assisting the chief motive of the picture.

For pure melodious beauty perhaps there is no plate like 20. "There were not found women fair as the daughters of Job in all the land, and their father gave them inheritance among their brethren." Job is seated in a dim rich chamber, on whose walls are wrought paintings illustrating the trials he has experienced.[Pg 157] Around him are grouped three beautiful daughters, who listen rapt while he relates to them God's dealings with him.

This is a rare example of Blake's choosing an interior with no opening out into the beyond. It is quaint and beautiful, but we are so accustomed to seeing Blake's figures set in the open air with the sky above them, that this closed-in chamber, exquisitely wrought and fantastic as it is, seems a thing foreign to his usual methods, his elective affinity for the great expansive types of God's universe. I think the reason he chose an interior in this instance was that we might be shut in and enclosed within the mind of Job as it revealed itself to his daughters. Instinctively we know that Blake's true lover Rossetti must have cared for this plate with quite special fervour, so close is the analogy between its hidden mysterious richness and the wonderful painted interiors in which he set his women, and from which he developed such a high degree of romantic suggestion and atmosphere. A lute and harp amid trailing vines, grape-laden, form a border to Blake's design, as delicate as the illuminated tracery in a mediaeval Hour-Book. In the final plate—"So the Lord blessed the latter end of Job more than the beginning"—the hole of the great tree that has figured in so many of the designs is surrounded by a crowd of persons, with Job, his wife and beautiful daughters in the midst. All play on instruments of music, while sheep and lambs and (it must be admitted) a most Gothic-looking sheep-dog repose in the immediate foreground. The ancient and fantastic instruments, the rapt upraised faces, the beautiful girls, recall the old Florentine singing galleries—cantorias as they are called—the one by Donatello and the other by Luca della Robbia, now in the Museo del Duomo at Florence. In neither has the joy of praise, the delight in making music, found more complete expression.

[Pg 158]Blake's "Book of Job" is a holy thing. The full compass of his orchestral nature exerted itself for this final effort. All his long sacrifices, deprivations, passionate sorrows and sacred joys, his burning aspirations and his steadfast faith, found their true meaning, their perfect consecration in the blossoming of this supreme flower on his tree of life. It was Blake's offering to God, like the Sacred Host, reserved and offered up in his own hands on the altar of his storm-weary heart.

CHAPTER XI
WORK IN THE EXHIBITION OF 1904

In the January of 1904 Messrs. Carfax's tiny galleries at 17, Ryder Street, St. James's, became a shrine to which all pious lovers of William Blake hastened to make their pilgrimage. None of the usual crowd that visit picture shows were to be descried here.

Blake's appreciators are not those who are most learned in schools of painting, in tricks of style and niceties of technique. They are mainly composed of those who, having a strong pictorial sense, are yet only effectively moved by *ideas* in art.

And what a harvest of ideas was garnered here!—ideas which sprung like Athene fully developed and armed from the head of Blake—of which head a cast taken by Deville the phrenologist was conspicuously placed in the centre of the lower room of the exhibition. The closely-set mouth and jaw, arched and inflated nostrils, massy brow, and intense and rapt expression, tell one something of the nature of this rare and spiritual intellect.

Out of forty-one exhibits, twenty-five were subjects from the Bible, three were single plates repeated from Blake's "Prophetic Books," one was an Indian ink drawing illustrating a scene in his poem "Tiriel," three were purely imaginative compositions, the keys to which were to be sought in themselves, and seven were illustrations to the poets (three of Milton's "Paradise Lost," one of a scene in Shakespeare's "Midsummer Night's Dream,"[Pg 160] and three sketches to illustrate Gray, Young, and Blair). Mainly, then, the exhibition might be said to have dealt with Biblical subjects, though good specimens of all kinds of Blake's work rendered it representative of his genius in its various phases.

From the old Byzantine mosaicists through art's early springtime to her full summer in the Renaissance, and even since then, no class of subjects has so deeply occupied the mind of painters as sacred history. There are no incidents left untreated in the New Testament, and the Old has had a large meed of attention, yet we find a painter of such unique and peculiar genius as William Blake expending his strength and invention on this well-worn field of motives. But with results so new, so different from anything ever achieved before, that our interest and delight were stimulated in proportion to our susceptibility to Blake's influence. I am not saying that this new treatment of Biblical subjects, of the Gospel story, is finer than the work of the old masters of the golden age of Italy. Nor do I rank it lower. "The ages are all equal," Blake says himself, "but genius is always above its age." The great point is that it is entirely *different*, and that it exhibits a total disregard for traditional treatment. Blake only found it *possible* to see these subjects from his own point of view—one never before attained by any artist. And as objects seen from different outlooks vary in colour, profile, and proportion, so as to be sometimes quite unrecognizable, so do these religious pictures of Blake's appear startlingly alien to any we have ever seen before. Or as he puts it himself, "If perceptive organs vary, objects of perception seem to vary too."

Looking round the characteristic and representative collection, the ingenuous student realized that the predominant effect of this art on his mind was one of *strangeness*. It seemed to him unconnected with the[Pg 161] past, unrelated to the present, an art set apart, unique, somewhat disquieting, which took him into Blake's visionary world, opposed in every sense to the natural world of daily experience. This visionary world of Blake's, was minutely discriminated by him, however, and was no formless region of emasculating dreams.

The amazing vigour of his conceptions, and the flat contradiction which they impose on the orthodox and traditional images which most people's minds unconsciously harbour, added a sense of shock to that of strangeness. Inquiring yet further into the causes of this impression one discovered the truth of W. B. Scott's assertion, that Blake's genius was unaided by its usual correlative, talent—that facility which enthrones the idea in its appropriately wrought shrine, dowers it with its organically perfect form. Greatly as Blake disliked it to be said, the truth was apparent among these collected works of his, that his execution was seldom equal to his invention. As proof of the strangeness, the independence of his work, we may quote the water-colour drawing of the "Three Maries with the Angel at the Sepulchre" (date 1803), in which the holy women shrink terrified from the angel, with all the shuddering horror that humanity feels at the manifestations of the spiritual world. A small colour-print from "Urizen"—called here "The Flames of Furious Desire"—with which we are already very familiar, must have augmented the impression of unique imagination and strangeness to those who had no previous acquaintance with Blake's work.

The furious raging, the vital majesty of the water-colour called "Fire," the delicate and curious imagination in "Satan watching the Endearments of Adam and Eve," with many others must have contributed to this effect; but the final strangeness and most curious beauty were to be found in "The Nativity," The[Pg 162] River of Life," and "The Bard." In these, Blake's highest and most mystic qualities are manifest, and his divergence from all preconceived ideas startlingly apparent. "The Nativity" is a small tempera picture painted on copper without the usual foundation of gesso that Blake first laid on the plate. Small patches of tempera have been dislodged, showing little gleaming bits of copper, but happily this has occurred mainly at the top part of the picture in the gloom of the roof of the stable. All the long succession of Nativities from Giotto to Correggio ("the soft and effeminate and consequently most cruel demon," as Blake termed him) seem not to have touched his imagination. Most artists carry an "infused remembrance" of great pictures in their mind, and can seldom divest themselves of the subtle influence emanating therefrom. But Blake's picture is not in any sense a composition which even unconsciously has been built up with the aid of memory. Imagination has here become vision, the uncovering of the veritable image; and Blake has faithfully copied what his entranced consciousness beheld.

Mary, white as the lilies of her annunciation, has fallen back fainting into the arms of Joseph, while above her prostrate body, "a mist of the colour of fire" would seem to have gradually taken form and become incarnate in the exquisite beauty of the infant Jesus. Light as thistledown and shining like a star, so that the whole chamber—with the terrified Joseph, the white mother, the oxen feeding—are all illuminated by its intense radiance—this apotheosis of divinity in childhood takes flight to the outstretched arms of St. Elizabeth, who sits on the floor with a quaint little St. John praying in her lap. The open window through which is discerned the star in the East, takes the imagination out into the night of limitless mystery.

The technique is superior to most of Blake's work in[Pg 163] tempera, and is adequate, the rendering of light in the picture containing qualities nothing short of marvellous.

It was impossible to look at this "Nativity" without being moved. The event appeared to Blake entirely supernatural in effect as in cause. He seems to have attached no historical value to it, nor indeed to any of his Biblical subjects. They were to him merely symbols of eternal ideas, projected by the Holy Ghost into the world for its enlightenment, and of these ideas Christ was the chiefest; but every idea he thought capable of manifesting itself equally in diverse symbols. His mind had some of the contemplative and impersonal characteristics of the oriental, and by its original processes he was enabled to appreciate the true inwardness of Christianity as the western mind cannot do. Christianity was born in the East like the Star of its Epiphany, and has come to maturity in the West, but its most mystical secrets will be hid from us until it has returned again and bathed in the immemorial symbolism and true occultism of the East.

Being so unfortunate as not to obtain leave from the "Nativity's" present owner to reproduce it in these pages, I have been obliged to take our illustration from the etching which William Bell Scott made after the original, and for which permission was courteously granted me by Messrs. Chatto and Windus. It is but the shadow of a shadow, for Bell Scott's etching is only that, but it will serve to give some idea of the solemn beauty of the tempera painting.

Now let me recall another purely imaginative composition.

"The River of Life," a water-colour picture, reminded me in its transparence and delicate brilliance of Blake's earlier printed books.

It is a rhapsody of Heaven. The River of Life which flows through the City of God, and in which all [Pg 164]new-born souls are dipped, is a mighty stream flowing between green banks, on which are situated the gleaming houses of the city. Groups of happy souls wander beside the clear pale waters, and with his back towards us the Saviour with two children (new-born souls) in either hand swims towards the river's source, which is the Throne of God, typified by the sun. In its rays may be descried adoring angels, reminding us of Blake's ardent words, which I have already quoted, "What! it will be questioned, when the sun rises, do you not see a round disc of fire, somewhat like a guinea?" "Oh, no, no! I see an innumerable company of the heavenly host crying, 'Holy, holy, holy is the Lord God Almighty!'"

Two angels—angels of the presence—remain suspended in flight above the stream on either side, playing on pipes, while a beautiful strong woman, clad in lemon-yellow robe, swoops down like a bird just above the surface of the stream with lithe strenuous body bent to meet the wind. She is a delicious creation, satisfying the aesthetic sense with completeness. The disposition of the figures in this picture, the decorative arrangement of the overhanging fruit-laden branches of the Tree of Life, the clear treble notes of colour, made one think of the rare and iridescent art of Japan. Blake's mood when he painted "The River of Life" must have attained to a high and heavenly unity and joy.

"The Bard" is a picture of quite another order, and pitched in a very different key. Here is a twilight world of intellectual notions and poetic motives wafted hither and thither on the blast of the Bard's frenzy. The Bard himself, a commanding figure, stands on a shelf of rock surveying the vortex, while he smites music from his harp. Below, a king and queen and their horses are overwhelmed in a Stygian stream. All[Pg 165] is dark, with a strange gleam and shimmer here and there, like jewels and burnished silver seen through a purple veil. This was one of the pictures that appeared in Blake's own exhibition in his brother's shop, and his description in the celebrated catalogue is well worth quotation:

On	a	rock		whose		haughty	brow
Frown'd	o'er	old		Conway's		foaming	flood,
Robed	in	sable		garb		of	evil
With	haggard	eyes		the		Poet	stood:
Loose	his	beard		and		hoary	hair
Streamed	like	a	meteor	of	the	troubled	air.
Weave	the	warp	and	weave	the		woof,

The winding-sheet of Edward's race.

Thus the poet Gray; and Blake commented, "Weaving the winding-sheet of Edward's race by means of sounds of spiritual music, and its accompanying expressions of spiritual speech, is a bold and daring and most masterly conception that the public have embraced and approved with avidity.

"Poetry consists in these conceptions, and shall painting be confined to the sordid drudgery of facsimile representations of merely mortal and perishing substances, and not be as poetry and music are, elevated to its own proper sphere of invention and visionary conception? No, it shall not be so! Painting as well as poetry and music exists and exults in immortal thoughts.

"The connoisseurs and artists who have made objections to Mr. Blake's mode of representing spirits with real bodies would do well to consider that the Venus, the Minerva, the Jupiter, the Apollo, which they admire in Greek statues are all of them representations of spiritual existences—of gods immortal—to the ordinary perishing organ of sight; and yet they are embodied and organized in solid marble. Mr. Blake requires the[Pg 166] same latitude and all is well. King Edward and Queen Eleanor are prostrated with their horses at the foot of the rock on which the Bard stands—prostrated by the terrors of his harp, on the margin of the river Conway, whose waves bear up a corpse of a slaughtered bard at the foot of the rock. The armies of Edward are seen winding among the mountains.

He wound with toilsome march his long array!

"Mortimer and Gloucester lie spellbound behind the King. The execution of this picture is also in water-colours or fresco," he added finally. It was probably painted in water-colours with white of egg or glue on a medium of gesso. The gloomy glory of its colour was a thing to ponder on. Like the dim silvery splendour of a pearl seen in the twilight of deep-sea waters, so does it glint and gleam. In no picture has Blake brought home to us more directly the visible population of the world of his mind—its power and grandeur and mystery—than in the complex imagery of this great work.

The picture was probably painted in 1785, and was exhibited at the Royal Academy. It afterwards appeared again at Blake's own exhibition in 1809. It is a sad thing that he so seldom dated the pictures which he executed for his staunch friend and supporter Mr. Butts. The pictures in the Exhibition, with a very few exceptions, were originally done for him, but few of them could have an authentic date affixed to them. All Blake's original methods of working were here represented by splendid examples.

First there are the tempera pictures, or "frescoes," as he termed them. He would never paint in oil-colour, because he thought and wrote that "oil, being a body itself, will drink, or absorb very little colour, and changing yellow, and at length brown, destroys every colour it is mixed with, especially every delicate colour. It[Pg 167] turns every permanent white to a yellow or brown putty, and has compelled the use of that destroyer of colour, white lead, which when its protecting oil is evaporated will become lead again," and he hotly affirmed the opinion that "oil became a fetter to genius and a dungeon to art." This being so, he evolved a method of painting in water-colours, stiffened with white of egg or dilute glue, on a ground prepared with whiting or plaster and laid on copper or board.

When the "fresco" was finished he varnished it with a preparation of glue. In his old age Linnell lent him a copy of Cennino Cennini's "Trattato della pittura," and he was delighted to find that the method he had always employed in his tempera pictures was very like that of the old sixteenth-century painter.

Occasionally his pictures acquired the mellow harmony, the indescribable deep, yet faded tenderness of the old masters' tempera pictures, as for instance that entitled "Bathsheba at the Bath seen by David." There is nothing supernatural or weird here, save the flowers which grow around the pool, and they are like the strange mysterious blooms that appear to one in dreams. Bathsheba, nude and beautiful, with her two childish attendants, one on either side, somehow recalls the work of Masaccio and Filippino Lippi in the Chapel of the Carmine at Florence, perhaps because it is so nobly naturalistic in treatment.

Another beautiful tempera is "The Flight into Egypt." It was painted in 1790—the year of the "Marriage of Heaven and Hell." Holman Hunt developed in his magnificent picture of the same subject a poetic motive first used by Blake. The great may take from the great without shame. The angelic spirits of the martyred Innocents flutter around the Mother and Child, while the ass on which they ride is followed by angels with great gloomy wings, like night made visible and [Pg 168]beneficent. The Virgin's little delicate face looks wistfully from the dim picture like one of Gentile da Fabbriano's small jewel-clear miniatures, and a crescent moon shines vaguely silver through the darkness. This is a picture of high and tender imaginative quality, more in the spirit of old masters like Fra Angelico, it must be admitted, than characteristically Blakean in expression.

There are three other methods used by Blake, of which one—the printed or engraved outline, filled in with hand-wrought water-colour—is so familiar to us from the examples studied at the British Museum, that we need not linger to describe it again. At the British Museum we have also seen many of Blake's "colour-printed" designs, but not any nearly as fine as the two pictures entitled "Hecate" and "Lamech and his two Wives" of the exhibition. The process, according to the younger Tatham's account, was as follows: "Blake when he wanted to make his prints in oil, took a common thick millboard and drew, in some strong ink or colour, his designs upon it strong and thick. He then painted upon that in such oil colours and on such a state of fusion that they would blur well. He painted roughly and quickly, so that no colour would have time to dry. He then took a print of that on paper, and this impression he coloured up in water-colours, repainting his outline on the millboard when he wanted to take another impression; and each having a sort of accidental look, he could branch out so as to make each one different. The accidental look they had was very enticing."

The depth and grandeur of tone obtained in "Hecate" are unique, and, united to the sombre majesty of the composition, form a most satisfying work to eye and intellect. Looking closely at the technique, the colour is seen to be collected in little pin-head dots all over the ground, in a manner that clearly points to its having[Pg 169] been impressed while yet wet, with some carefully roughened surface, but just what means were used to obtain this effect must always remain a mystery.

The finest example of the process is, however, "Lamech and his two Wives," in which the tragic nature of the subject is deepened by the colour-printing, here most successfully handled.

Pure water-colour, sometimes delicately outlined with the pen, was Blake's fourth mode of working, and the exhibition had a goodly array of this class of work. We have mentioned "The River of Life," perhaps the most beautiful example extant, but several others, noticeably "Oberon, Titania, and Puck with fairies dancing" and "The Wise and Foolish Virgins," were very lovely. The first represents Blake in a rare mood, his mysticism in abeyance, and his temper one of aesthetic abandon. We are so little accustomed to think of him as an artist of varied and wide appeal, that this rhythmic dance, which acted on the spectator like music, surprised. It has in it the delirious joy of elemental things. The fairies' delicate muslins are fetched out like mist in the greenwood; butterflies' wings and petals of flower adorn their dainty heads. Puck has wings on the back of his hands (a new and delightful idea this!), and the rapid graceful movements of the dance do not seem to be arrested by their embodiment in a painting. Though this phase of Blake is distinctly novel, even strange to us, it is entirely delightful. There is no stress, no repelling yet attractive mystery as in the "Hecate" here. It is just pure "joie de vivre."

"The Wise and Foolish Virgins" is much more characteristic of him. The wise virgins in the foreground are ranged in a row, their lamps by their sides. Their bodies and faces are smitten with a cold unearthly white light, presumably, but not obviously, thrown by the lamps. The modelling of their forms is most careful.[Pg 170] Behind them, issuing from a small hut, the foolish virgins, in wild confusion, implore oil for their lamps. The landscape in which the scene is laid is anything but Eastern. Dark, intensely green downs undulate and swell to meet the sky. A lurid light defines the horizon, and in the swathed masses of gray cloud above, an angel blowing a trump (suggesting a Last Judgement) wings his fateful way. It may easily be urged (and the prosaic mind which only rejoices in the precise and neat imitation of what it can *see* is sure to exclaim) that here is a defiance of all artistic rules, a pitiable inability to copy the most ordinary natural phenomena, proclaiming Blake a wilful "poseur" or an unobservant madman. "Here," they exclaim, "is little atmosphere, no distance, no attempt at truth of tone, and no comprehensible rendering of the light."

Blake rendered it as he did because he *chose*; because his masterly sense of style (that is, the treatment best suited to the representation of the idea, his subjective vision) required it to be so painted and thus only, because he considered himself free to take from Nature just what he needed for his purpose, and never felt himself obliged to make an entire and wholly truthful representation of her. To emphasize the light on the figures of the foreground, he overcharged the colour in the sky and the downs behind, and by this treatment obtained an effect productive of strange and solemn emotion in the beholder.

Nature was to him shadow or reminiscence only, and here he has defiantly subordinated the truth of the landscape to the spiritual truth of his subject.

The most significant types were revealed in his soul, and owned a relationship to the visible creation only in so far as this relationship was necessary to render his art-work intelligible to the world. His decorative sense approved of the white virgins set so statue-pale against[Pg 171] the dark green of the downs. The suddenness of the contrast, the livid and supernatural effect, were part of his deliberate intention. So does the white fire of an intense spiritual alertness contrast with the opaque darkness of natural physical life. For this scene, taken from the parable of Jesus, is only another of those types which Blake regarded in so wide and catholic a sense, and which by his treatment he has lifted above all merely historical association into a realm of pure spiritual symbolism.

The pleasure derived from the examination of his collected pictures is rather that of a profound intellectual excitement than a purely aesthetic satisfaction. The climax of this excitement is reached before the two pictures called, respectively, "Elohim creating Adam" and "Satan triumphing over Eve." How different is Blake's conception of the former subject to Michael Angelo's, and yet, widely different as they are, somehow we know them to be related. Elohim, in the vortex of the winds, lifts a face pale with awe and power, as he calls into being from the clay below him a figure scarcely human yet, and stamped with the stamp of terrestrial creeping mortality. A snake binds one leg, and there is no other suggestion of life about this half-developed repelling organism. But presently Elohim will breathe into the clay, and then this thing (which somehow recalls Mrs. Shelley's "Frankenstein" to my shuddering fancy!) will arise and live.

Michael Angelo chose the right moment, the body made beautiful but languid, and God's finger applied like a magnet to the limp hand through which the fiery currents of life are just beginning to flow in thrilling gushes into the perfect body. But Blake, with a more curious care for the earlier part of the process of creation, a more meditative and less dramatic sense, invites us to dwell on, not the final perfect beauty of created man,[Pg 172] but his partial evolution from the dark earth to which he will one day return. The accidental character of the body of man, the universal nature of the Spirit of God, without whose inspiration there is no beauty nor comeliness—these are thoughts on which he mused while painting this great and terrible picture.

The death-weary figure of Eve in the companion picture was a haunting thing. Overcome by the serpent's wiles, Eve lies prostrate in the tightening coils, and the cruel flat head is pressed upon the white breast, whose power to resist is quite gone. The struggle is over, the delicate body is relaxed, the little head has fallen back piteously, and the eyes are closed, for no blue heavens smile comfort down on her who lies so low in the dust. Satan in clouds of terror triumphs above her, and her overthrow is complete.

A little sketch in pencil, ink and wash, called "Satan, Sin and Death," has a human figure (strangely enough that of Satan), finely posed, and drawn with infinite power. The vigorous torso, slender hips, fine and muscular legs, are classic in their heroic proportions, but it must be admitted that the inspiration of the sketch as a whole is below Blake's level.

I must notice a very fine and highly-finished water-colour, called "The Judgment of Paris." The subject was a congenial one to Blake, who entertained the most original notions about classic legend and literature. He wrote in the Descriptive Catalogue:

"The Artist (Blake) having been taken in vision into the ancient republics, monarchies, and patriachates of Asia, has seen those wonderful originals called in the sacred scriptures the Cherubim, which were sculptured and painted on walls of temples, towers, cities, palaces, and erected in the highly-cultivated States of Egypt, Moab, Eden, Arum among the rivers of Paradise—being the originals from which the Greeks and Hetruvians[Pg 173] copied Hercules Farnese, Venus of Medicis, Apollo Belvedere, and all the grand works of ancient art....

"No man can believe that either Homer's Mythology or Ovid's was the production of Greece or Latium; neither will anyone believe that the Greek statues, as they are called, were the invention of Greek artists; perhaps the Torso is the only original work remaining, all the rest being evidently copies, though fine ones, from the greater works of the Asiatic patriarchs. The Greek muses are daughters of Mnemosyne or Memory, and not of Inspiration or Imagination, therefore not authors of such sublime conceptions."

In this ingenious way did Blake seek to justify his admiration for the old pagan art, the old pagan mythology. They were recollections of symbols and ideas given by God to the ancient patriarchs of the Old Testament, and from them had filtered through to the civilization of Greece and Rome. To Blake it all amounted to this, "God hath not left Himself without witnesses," and he vehemently protested against any race, age, or religion arrogating to itself the authorship of ideas which should only be ascribed to God.

So that the "Judgment of Paris" is treated like the biblical subjects, as a spiritual parable. When the apple of desire is given to mere sensual beauty instead of to moral or intellectual beauty, Love, the winged spirit, flies away, and Discord, the malformed demon, arrives. The three goddesses' forms, delicate as reeds, pure as Blake's austere imagination, and modelled with tender care for their lovely limbs, hands and faces, awaken in us a great wonder at the technique he could command when he chose. One of the tenderest and most beautiful of Blake's slightly tinted drawings, "The Vision of Queen Katherine"—we are enabled to reproduce through the kindness of its present owner, Sir Charles Dilke. The composition is of exceeding harmony, the[Pg 174]delicate outlines being suave, fluent, gracious, to a singular degree. Sweetness and tenderness are its predominant characteristics, and it is without a rival among Blake's works in this respect, saving perhaps for the picture, "And when they had sung an hymn they ascended unto the Mount of Olives."

Katherine, sick unto death, has been soothed to sleep by music:

Cause	the	musicians	play	me	that	sad	note
I	named	my	knell,	whilst	I	sit	meditating

On that celestial harmony I go to,

she had asked. Griffith and Patience sit beside her, unconscious of the vision that is blessing her sleep. Katherine, beautiful and crowned, "makes in her sleep signs of rejoicing, and holdeth up her hands to heaven." Angels of diminutive but exquisite forms float in circles above her, and two are holding a crown of laurels over her head. Many pictures—the Indian ink drawing called "The Deluge," an infinite waste of stormy sea; "The Entombment," a picture of solemn intensity and originality; and others deserve description and comment, but space does not allow.

The exhibition was an occasion of much illumination to Blake's admirers, and the thoughts on his art which it gave rise to may be happily summarized in a passage from Heine's "Salon":

"Art attains its highest value when the symbol, apart from its inner meaning, delights our senses externally, like the flowers of a *selam*, which without regard to their secret signification are blooming and lovely, bound in a bouquet."

"But is such concord always possible? Is the artist so completely free in choosing and binding his mysterious flowers? Or does he only choose and bind together what he must? I affirm this question of mystical [Pg 175]un-freedom or want of will. The artist is like that somnambula princess who plucked by night in the garden of Bagdad, inspired by the deep wisdom of love, the strangest flowers, and bound them into a *selam*, of whose meaning she remembered nothing when she awoke. There she sat in the morning in her harem, and looked at the *bouquet de nuit*, musing on it as over a forgotten dream, and finally sent it to the beloved Caliph. The fat eunuch who brought it greatly enjoyed the beautiful flowers without suspecting their meaning. But Haroun al Raschid, the commander of the faithful, the follower of the Prophet, the possessor of the ring of Solomon, he recognized the deep meaning of the beautiful bouquet; his heart bounded with delight; he kissed every blossom, and laughed till tears ran down his long beard." We may not be followers of the Prophet, nor rejoice in long beards or magic rings, yet I dare assert that in entering into the meaning, the deep *"Innigkeit"* of the *selam* which Blake presented to us, we have entered on a new phase of spiritual and artistic life not less intensely delightful than the joy experienced by the Prophet.

[Pg 176]

CHAPTER XII
ENGRAVINGS AND DRAWINGS IN THE PRINT ROOM

I am afraid that the first view of Blake's engraving of "The Canterbury Pilgrimage" will prejudice the spectator unfavourably towards our artist, even if the work by him already seen has made its fascination felt.

Especially will this prejudice be heightened if the engraving from Stothard's picture of the same subject be set against Blake's and compared with it, for Blake's astonishes and repels on first sight, while Stothard's pleases at once.

In Stothard's composition the variety of the company, and especially of the horses they ride, is charming. Very different are the grim ranks of Blake's procession, the ten horses therein exhibiting only three positions among them, and those positions being all traditionally faithful to the hobby-horse type. Stothard's motley throng are gracefully habited, and appear dainty and spruce in spite of the dust of the highway as they amble along. His lighting of the picture, the firm and effective modelling of the horses and their riders, the wide range of tones amounting almost to colour itself, give a satisfying richness which we fail to find in Blake's picture.

The whole composition is harmonious, and for those who desire nothing further of art than that it shall cater for the eye without much or intimate reference to the mind, then Stothard's graceful performance is indeed pre-eminent.

[Pg 177]Turning to Blake's picture, we find he has catered for the mind, but, having done that, he has denied us the one thing of which Stothard is so prodigal—beauty. In his restless search beneath the surface with which beauty obviously is concerned, for the things of the spirit and the intelligence underlying the appearance, Blake has here lost sight of art's first principle, beauty in the whole, as the result of the parts. The composition in its entirety is not beautiful. It has no harmony. It is an accretion of separate parts, made out without reference to the picture's final unity. These parts, although some are beautiful in themselves, are not intimately related to each other, and contribute so little towards a general predominant scheme that the effect of discord is produced, and the multitudinous meanings and intentions with which each figure is fraught over-weight the composition and confuse the beholder; the simple reason of all this being, that the first obligation of the painter, his sense of harmony and balance, has been ruthlessly violated. Perhaps Blake's sense of style—about which I imagine he never reasoned, it being innate and intuitive—deserted him on this one occasion, because anger was making havoc in his heart and blinding his eyes. The conditions under which he worked, it will be remembered, must have been destructive to all concentration and artistic isolation of mood. Still, as I have said, though sadly wanting as a whole, there is beauty of an intricate and curious sort in the details.

Look on the wide expanse of swelling downs over-arched by the tragic splendour of an evening sky. Here the thought, as ever with Blake, is lifted up above the accidents, into the eternal and the infinite. But Stothard's gentle hills and bowery trees shut out such vistas, and he concerns himself scarcely at all about the sky, which is merely the background on which to[Pg 178] throw up the graceful heads of his graceful unintelligent folk.

The characteristic group of children with their mother and grandfather, which Blake has set beside the gateway of the Tabard Inn, has great beauty as a single motive. No labour has been spared to make all faithful to the Chaucerian conception: the curious semi-Gothic gateway, the crowding pigeons, the barbaric splendours of the wife of Bath, the mediaeval figure of the knight, whose face reminds one somewhat of the supposed portrait of Cimabue in the Chapel of the Spaniards in Santa Maria Novella; all have been wrought with painful care. The work is an illustration of Blake's principle enunciated in his notes on Reynolds' "Discourses" and elsewhere that "Real effect is making out of parts, and it is nothing else but that."

Perhaps the strangest trait the engraving exhibits in comparison with Stothard's is that it looks so antique. It might have been executed a hundred years earlier than the other picture, so wilfully grotesque and archaic is it. Yes, *wilfully* is the word, for Blake *wished* to make his procession as stiff and quaint and rich as the stately Chaucerian language that first painted the scene, forgetting perhaps that the two arts of poetry and painting achieve the same end through widely different conditions, and according to processes contiguous, but non-interchangeable. The want of ease, of careless and familiar naturalism in the engraving, may recall to those who look for it the splendid and ceremonious language of the old story-teller. The description written by Blake of his own design (it will be found in Gilchrist) shows how he loved and understood Chaucer, and, we may add, how very loosely the poem was grasped, and with what want of truth to the original it was represented by his rival. Lamb said of the engraving itself[Pg 179] that it was "a work of wonderful power and spirit, hard and dry, yet with grace," and the Descriptive Catalogue—a copy of which was given him by Crabb Robinson—pleased him greatly; the part devoted to an analysis of the characters in the "Canterbury Pilgrimage" he found to be "the finest criticism of Chaucer's poem he had ever read."

Savagely powerful as it is, the engraving is merely an interesting and not a vital utterance of Blake. The tempera picture from which it was engraved was bought by Mr. Butts, but has been lost sight of now for many years. Stothard's oil painting of the same subject is in the National Gallery.

Turning to the other original single engravings of Blake in the Print Room, we find several of interest. There is that early one, designed and engraved in 1780, which has been called "Glad Day," and is the expression of a mood oftener felt in Blake's early manhood than in the ensuing years of chafing complexity and multitudinous emotions. I have wondered whether it be not the pictorial embodiment of the vision which he saw of the "Spiritual Sun on Primrose Hill," described by him to Crabb Robinson.

Among the original engravings here may be seen the broadsheet of "Little Tom the Sailor," executed by Blake for Hayley while at Felpham in 1800, for a charitable purpose.

Hayley's verses and Blake's designs were bitten in with stopping-out varnish on the pewter plate of the original from which the prints are taken.

In the designs setting out the misfortunes of a poor widow and the heroism of her little son he has given us one theme of natural scenery—a winding path, a little wood surmounted by bare folded downs—testifying to the invasion which the obvious beauty of Felpham had made on his artistic consciousness; while[Pg 180] the other illustration represents the tragic moment when little Tom on the wreck is about to be drowned; over the trough of deep sea the spiritual form of his father appears ready to receive and embrace his soul. Mrs. Blake's hand unfortunately has coloured the Print Room copy.

And now let us turn to the pen-and-ink etchings to Dante, designed and executed for Mr. Linnell between the years 1824 and 1827, the year of Blake's death.

There are seven of them, wrought by the pen, which had become so deliberate, careful and delicate in execution during these last years of his life.

Let us linger over two of them for a moment.

Among the many pictures of Paolo and Francesca that exist, was there ever seen anything like this of Blake's imagining?

You may prefer others—Ary Scheffer's, Dante Rossetti's, or Mr. G. F. Watts'—you may object that this one has not grappled with the passionate love-motive of the story, that it has omitted the note of yearning, of beloved pain, with which Dante's conception is fraught. The austerity of a mind which theorized much on the subject of love—the love of man and woman—but knew actually very little of its vehemence, its trouble, and its languorous sweetness, forbade Blake to focus in the figures of Paolo and Francesca the ideal tragedy of those "whom love bereav'd of life."

The scene as a whole—that second circle of the Inferno, in which

The		stormy		blast	of	hell
With	restless	fury	drives	the	spirits	on,
Whirl'd		round	and		dashed	amain
With sore annoy—						

was what arrested his imagination. Here, in his rendering of the subject, the blast has torn upward in a visible ribbon-like vortex from the surface of the waters, bearing[Pg 181] within it, as images in a crystal, the innumerable figures of the world's great lovers. From a spit of land, Paolo and Francesca, fluttering "light before the wind," appear in a single tongue of flame, and Dante lies stretched upon the ground—"through compassion fainting." Virgil is seen irradiated by the effulgent light which trembles around the disc wherein the immortal kiss—that which Rostand calls "l'instant d'infini"—is poetically represented.

As usual, the force, the unusualness of the conception, rather than its ideal beauty are the points we notice first. But closer study attests to its beauty too. Mere literary interest would give the picture no real claim to artistic regard. But Blake felt the drawing of each bounding line as a thing of beauty in itself, having an aesthetic element of its own, apart from its representative or symbolic use. In that coil of entangled fates, what manifold themes of pure sensuous beauty are to be found! For instance—just at the leap and bend of the circle—appears a woman with arms extended in the fluent wind, like a bird in flight, and a man's embrace encircles her neck—a man whose face she kisses rapturously. Leaping, floating, falling, the multitudinous figures are borne onward by the resistless force of that terrible blast; and, however foreign or antipathetic this embodiment of Dante's vision may seem to us, we are bound to admit that its imaginative scope is of a temper characteristic not only of Blake, but of the Florentine himself. An aspect of Dante's conception is developed and emphasized here in a manner which has not been attempted in any other picture of the subject.

The other pen-and-ink drawing from the "Inferno" represents Dante and Virgil in the Circle of the Traitors, with the head of Bocca degli Abati breaking through the lake of ice at the foot of Dante. Blake has given[Pg 182] strangely passionless faces to his Dante and Virgil, but the pure simple lines of their figures are severely congruous with the scene, and the iceberg, formed of shadowy frozen figures to the right, is powerfully suggested by a few lines of sufficient economy. The picture is another of those unique embodiments from which, once seen and dwelt on, the modern imagination can never release itself. Gustave Doré's sensational rendering of the same scene seems to me to acknowledge an inspiration at this source.

The other five designs to Dante merit a description and attention which space does not allow us to give them here. They are of great power, but whether the unflinching realization of the terrible imaginings of Dante is permissible in pictorial art—where the visual representation attacks the emotions and intellect with a poignancy that words, however forcible, can never attain—is a question the discussion of which may provide food for argument to critics of the school of Lessing. For my own part, I incline to the opinion that they overstep the bounds of terror authorized in art, and approach the confines of the horrible in the treatment of the main motive of each design—"Admirably horrid," Mr. W. M. Rossetti pronounces them. The unwavering truth to Dante's detailed descriptions is beyond question, however.

The inmost sanctuary of an artist's mind is far more accessible through his pencil sketches than through his final consummated pictures and designs. There is something so intimate, so personal in these manifestations of himself, that in regarding them I have something of the feeling of one who listens unseen to a man thinking aloud. Nothing convinces one of the labour, the thought, the balancing, the rejections, the careful choice, that go to make up a picture like the study of the sketches made for it.

[Pg 183]The peculiarity of Blake's pencil sketches is their vehemence, and the absence in them of all hesitation. He seems from the first moment of conception to know exactly what he means to do, and rough, almost hieroglyphic, as the first shadow of his idea may appear at first sight, we have only to compare it with the design or picture which eventually resulted from it, to see that all the rapid "short-hand" lines of the sketch, block out accurately the disposition of the main parts of the design, the final attitude of the figures therein, without as a rule any real variation from the first idea having taken place in the working out.

This testifies more than anything else to the distinctness of the vision seen by Blake, and his eager passionate discernment of it. Among such sketches of clearly apprehended vision is that for "The Soul exploring the recesses of the Grave," the final design of which we are already very familiar with. It is executed with a broad-ended chalk pencil, in quick unhesitating lines. There is not a single touch that cannot be traced, that is not an essential development, in the finished picture, so that we know Blake saw it all from the first, complete then in his mind's eye as on the day when he finished the detailed drawing for the engraver.

Another sketch of the same order is one which, although it does not belong to any public collection, is so important as to excuse a reference to it here. Through the great kindness of Mr. Frederick Shields, to whom it belongs, I am enabled to reproduce it. The two motives of the picture in Blair's "Grave," called "Death's Door," had been favourite ones with Blake, and used by him separately in "The Gates of Paradise," "The Marriage of Heaven and Hell," and "America," before he combined them so felicitously in the noble design which ranks among his best works. The sketch by Blake belonging to Mr. Shields would seem to represent[Pg 184] the moment when he first realized the power and significance and beauty to be obtained by their incorporation in one design. Of this conception it must be admitted that it grew in Blake's mind after the first flashing vision of it, and was not from the beginning discernible in all the splendour to which it was eventually developed.

Here is another beautiful and careful sketch of a female figure diving through the air. The force of her perpendicular flight, the attitude of one leg (the left, not the right, however) recall the "Reunion of the Soul and the Body," but this figure is undraped, and the arms are extended downwards, and indeed the differences are so numerous that it cannot be regarded as a sketch for that picture. In all probability it is a preliminary study for one of the numerous figures in the "Last Judgment" which he executed for the Countess of Egremont in 1807.

Looking at the terse expressive little drawing, we are reminded of Blake's "golden rule of art"—"that the more distinct, sharp, and wiry the boundary line, the more perfect the work of art." Ah! but how he played with his line! "Wiry" at least it never was, say what Blake would! He never "painted" it, but felt his way along with sympathetic accuracy. And with what infinite inflexions of tenderness and strength did his pencil impress itself on the paper, indicating by that rare quality of touch more than form and modelling—almost, one had said—the very nature of the flesh of the figures he drew.

Speaking of Blake's drawings, the manner in which he drew the muscular form of the male leg is very noticeable and strangely characteristic of him. Another line he felt very tenderly was the curved sweep of a woman's back from shoulder to indented waist, and downwards to delicate ankles and heels.

[Pg 185]Let us linger a minute over another of what I may call Blake's shorthand sketches in the Print Room collection. It is undoubtedly the first idea for the picture entitled "The Spiritual form of Nelson guiding Leviathan, in whose wreathings are enfolded the nations of the earth." The finished picture appeared in Blake's own exhibition in 1809; it is now in the possession of T. W. Jackson, Esq., of Worcester College, Oxford.

In the sketch, "Nelson" is drawn symbolically as a young sea-god, nude and commanding. He stands firmly on a coil of Leviathan's body, which rearing and circling surrounds him like a frame. We can just distinguish the human forms caught in the serpent's toils, and its great mouth is in the act of devouring a man. The mouth is bridled, and the reins held by Nelson's hand. The symbolism is easy enough to understand and requires no explanation.

A carefully shaded and conscientious drawing of a naked man with arms upraised testifies to the fact that Blake *did* work from the model sometimes. But how cold such work appears— valuable and necessary as it is—compared with the passionate half-defined sketches, the mood of which transfers to us something of the high pleasure that Blake himself felt in making these burning transcripts from his imagination or visions.

I had much ado to make out the subject of the pen-and-wash sketch of a woman and man with a group of people on their knees in a cornfield. In the distance a thunder-cloud emits a lightning flash. Mr. Shields tells me that he and Dante Gabriel Rossetti spent an evening trying to decipher a larger and more definite sketch of the same idea, and finally decided that it was an illustration of the following verses (1 Sam. xii. 16-19): "Now therefore stand and see this great thing which the Lord will do before your eyes. Is it not wheat harvest to-day? I will call unto the Lord and[Pg 186] he shall send thunder and rain; that ye may perceive and see that your wickedness is great, which ye have done in the sight of the Lord, in asking you a king. So Samuel called unto the Lord, and the Lord sent thunder and rain that day; and all the people greatly feared the Lord and Samuel."

Among the many other sketches which space does not permit me to comment on, are two very beautiful studies in red chalk, showing Blake to be a master of line indeed. Of his engravings after designs by Stothard, Romney, Flaxman, Hogarth, examples of which the Print Room possesses, it is not necessary to speak, for this book is not concerned with engraving or any other technical branch of art. Its purpose is merely to examine into, and if possible lay bare, the nature of the artistic impulse that makes the work of Blake—as we may all know it in our public collections—so rare and so precious a thing. But though we shall not concern ourselves with these engravings, as they contribute nothing to our purpose, it is interesting to look at the numerous copies which our artist made from prints of Michael Angelo's frescoes on the roof of the Sistine, from drawings after the antique, and from Cumberland's "Designs for Engravings." These latter are pen drawings of Greek figures—similar to those represented on old black and yellow vases—and display the Greek ideal of form, so beautiful yet so passionless and un-individual, when compared with the figures of the great Florentine, in which the soul with all its struggles is apparent. Copying such diverse work faithfully—"for," wrote Blake, "servile copying is the great merit of copying"—must have made him think, compare, choose. Goethe says that his study of the ancient classic literature convinced him "that a vast abundance of objects must lie before us ere we can think upon them,—that we must accomplish something, nay, fail in something,[Pg 187] before we can learn our own capacities and those of others." And this was much more the case with Blake and his art than might be supposed. It was not ignorance of other ideals, of other methods of thought and work, that caused him to take the artistic path he did; it was definite choice, the ratification of his innate, strongly individualistic tendencies, resulting from comparing them with the characteristic principles of art exhibited in other ages, other masters. Blake in fact copied a good deal; he himself writes in his notes on Reynolds, "the difference between a bad artist and a good one is: the bad artist seems to copy a great deal, the good one really does copy a great deal."

Turning to his water-colour sketches in the Print Room, I consider the finest to be a very portrait-like head of an old man. It was evidently put in in pencil and pale washes of colour, and afterwards strengthened, rather daringly, with pen-and-ink outlines. The face with its deep eyes and noble contours is that of a seer, awestruck before his vision. It is in such work as this—swift, strong and delicate—that we see Blake at his best. In finished work—such little as he has left us—some heat, some fire seems to have escaped, but in sketches such as this the inspiration is contained in all its strongly-spiced vitality; that which is left undone, assisting that which is done, in producing an impression of energy and imaginative development. A pale-tinted, very careful and elaborate drawing of the Whore of Babylon, as Blake imagined her, next claims our attention. It was etched and reproduced by William Bell Scott. Never did Blake represent so voluptuous, so sensual a face, as this of the Whore of Babylon, which in spite of its beauty is of the same type as that of the Wife of Bath in his "Canterbury Pilgrimage." In its expression it has no fellow, save perhaps the face of Leda in Michael Angelo's small statuette in the Bargello.[Pg 188]The woman is seated on a seven-headed semi-human monster, and she holds in her hand a cup out of which smoke issues and condenses in the forms of floating men and women of incomparable grace. These swim around her head in a long ribbon-like streamer, and as the little figures reach the ground they are devoured by the seven heads. They symbolize the pleasures, ambitions, lusts of this world.

Another beautiful water-colour, in faint and tender colour, is perhaps the very vignette for Blair's "Grave," which Blake sent to Cromek with his verses of dedication to the Queen, and which was returned on his hands with such a cruel and insulting letter. Part of this design has been etched and reproduced by William Bell Scott. A mother and her young family, from whose ankles the chains of mortality have just been severed, ascend upward with looks of solemn exaltation on their rapt faces. They form a noble group. Above, on the left, is an angel with a sword and key who has presumably just set them free; he is Death, I suppose—a young and beautiful Death; while to the right is another Apollo-like being, who holds a pair of scales and represents St. Michael. In the most ancient Italian pictures the Archangel is often pictured as weighing the souls of the newly dead.

A large and very important water-colour drawing is called the "Lazar House," from Milton. It is one of Blake's terrible works, and has a tendency to haunt the memory unpleasantly. It is very powerful.

A great blind, bearded figure, with outstretched arms—Death in another aspect—is suspended in air over a scene of painfulness and intense horror, such as few artists would dare to represent. The victims of plague are writhing in death-agonies on the floor, while a figure to the right, with sinister face and nervous hand clutching a bolt (or is it a knife?), fills the spectator with[Pg 189] insane shudderings and alarm. He eyes the sufferers with gloating satisfaction, and the fact that he is coloured green as verdigris from head to foot does not detract from his horrible fascinations. I can never get over the feeling that pictures such as these caused Blake profound pain, that indeed he sought relief from their dominion over his mental life by turning the vision that haunted him into a definite artistic image, thus by the act of projection getting rid of the disquieting, the torturing inward tyrant. For with him, as I have striven to show, all thought came with the definiteness of vision; so that he could not read Milton's or Dante's descriptions without seeing the thing described, immediately start into visible being before him.

A finished and elaborate water-colour of a female recumbent figure on a tomb, with a foreground starred with brilliant flowers, is called "Letho Similis," but in no respect is it like Blake's work, and there seems no reason whatever to consider it as having been done by his hand, except that it has passed as his for a long time. So acute a critic as Mr. W. M. Rossetti casts doubt on the authorship of the work in his descriptive catalogue.

On the whole I think the review of Blake's pencil sketches and drawings impress one as powerfully as any of the work of his which we have previously seen, and mainly for the reason that it is in these that we can most clearly trace his thoughts in process of evolution.

And now all that remains for us to do is to visit the National Gallery, and there in the little octagonal room behind the Turner Gallery seek out those few precious works which are the representatives of his genius to the public at large. Whether that public often penetrates here, or, being here, lingers even momently before the few strange little pictures by Blake which it contains, may be questioned.

[Pg 190]That they are not popular, and that the little room is never crowded, needs no demonstration. Blake's greatness is not of the kind that can ever compete successfully with the claims of such masters as his contemporaries—Stothard, Romney, Gainsborough and Reynolds—whose brilliant and alluring work adorns the galleries through which one must pass to reach the little octagonal room where his few pictures, modestly retired behind the door, await such as will patiently seek them out.

First let us look at the water-colour numbered 43, entitled "David delivered out of Deep Waters." It has qualities of handling akin to the "River of Life," belonging to Captain Butts, and the conception is specially Blakean. David, with his arms bound round with cords, floats symbolically on dark waters. Above, seven cherubim, with wings interlacing like the shields of a phalanx, swoop down in rhythmic ranks, with Christ in their centre. The remarkable thing about these cherubim is that two have the faces of children, two those of old white-bearded men, two those of mature manhood, while the centre one alone, immediately below Christ, has the face of a beautiful youth.

The figure and attitude of the Saviour have a noble grace, but the face is weak and ineffectual, as is usual with Blake when treating the divine lineaments.

The effect of the picture—with those strong, ordered wings in ranks, recalling the banners borne in some rich church procession—is one of curious symmetry, of almost heraldic composition. A delicate and remote strangeness of imagination makes itself felt in every line, every tint; and the range of tone is noticeably peculiar, the deepest and highest parts of the scale being used with great effect, while no recourse has been had to the intermediate gamut, so that there is no full body of colour present at all. The nearest approach to it is the[Pg 191] quivering pale golden light that is diffused around the figure of Christ.

No. 1164, "The Procession from Calvary," is a tempera picture reminiscent in quality of colour of the *quattrocento* Italian masters. Stiff, composed and straight is the body of Jesus laid on the bier. Three pairs of bearers support the holy burden on their shoulders. The Virgin alone, and two other women side by side, follow the *cortége*, while in the distance Calvary, with its three crosses, may be seen; and Jerusalem is represented by a group of buildings defiantly Gothic in character. The bearers and the women moving across the foreground so majestically, so quietly, might be the somewhat stiff rendering of an idea, inspired by the procession in a basrelief on some old Greek or Roman sarcophagus, such as Mantegna or Andrea del Castagno worked out on canvas.

Then there is a highly-finished water-colour of an allegory—numbered 44—to be studied. It is soon evident to the spectator that the elaborate composition owns as central motive the Atonement, with all the symbolic correspondences which in the scriptures predicted it. At the highest point of the picture is a medallion wherein the Almighty is represented. Dull flames flicker and smoke around, while on them is inscribed in very small writing the significant words "God out of Christ is a consuming fire." This, as we know, was a much-insisted-on doctrine of Blake's, for he seems to have denied at times the responsible fatherhood of God; and never did he share the respectable conception of Him, prevalent at that day even more than in this, which Tennyson so aptly defined as "an immeasurable clergyman."

Below the medallion are little scenes displaying the Death of Abel, the Flood, the Sacrifice of Isaac, the Transfiguration, and, finally, the symbolic Vision of the[Pg 192] Holy Grail. All these separate but related motives are woven together, with subsidiary scenes to right and left, into one intricate and most beautiful scheme.

The low tones of the composition, the dim, delicate tinting, bring the varied and multitudinous parts into a harmony of effect that is very delightful, while the spiritual and intellectual material with which it is characteristically builded up, send our thoughts voyaging out like birds over the sea of religious mysticism.

I have left the most important picture to be dealt with last. The tempera picture, numbered 1110, was painted as the companion to "Nelson and Leviathan"—a sketch for which is in the British Museum, it will be remembered—and was shown for the first time at Blake's own exhibition in 1809. In his Descriptive Catalogue the title ran as follows: "The spiritual form of Pitt guiding Behemoth; he is that Angel, who, pleased to perform the Almighty's orders, rides on the whirlwind directing the storms of war; he is ordering the Reaper to reap the vine of the earth, and the Ploughman to plough up the cities and towers."

At first sight the figure of a beautiful young man is the one thing that stands out clearly from the dim splendour and bewildering detail of the picture. This noble form, instinct with power and authority, represents the spiritual body of Pitt. A gleaming halo surrounds his head, and the background is massed with seething indistinct figures.

Here and there strange glancing lights and phosphorescent stars emit a milky radiance, but it is some few minutes before the eye can distinguish the head and back of Leviathan. On either side of the great halo appears a man's form; one holds the crescent moon by way of sickle, the other presses heavily upon a harrow. They are the Reaper, Death, and the Ploughman Equality. All is steeped in gloomy twilight touched[Pg 193] here and there with subdued yet brilliant light, as of moonlight on water. Strange little figures seem to gather form out of the brownish mist before one's very eyes, and there is something of a miraculous charm on this cosmos—the fruit of the travail of Blake's intellect.

Of serenity, of clarity, there is none; but Blake's virtue, his quality with its necessary attendant defects, dominates this work and makes it precious in the sense of a unique record of a unique conception. Therefore it is fittingly placed as a representative of Blake's genius in our National Palace of Art.

What the place assigned to Blake by future generations will be is not for me to predict. That he has been gravely misapprehended and foolishly neglected until the last few years is common knowledge, but even to-day the ranks of his true lovers are scattered and few, though there are some people who affirm that an exaggerated distinction, an inflated value, attaches to his name at present, as a result of the swing of time's pendulum. Such people, however, are not among those who under any circumstances would be likely to admire Blake or appreciate his unique point of view.

This little book has had for its object, not the imparting of any new facts about him, nor the technical discussion of his works, but the reverent and sympathetic meditation on our own National Blake treasures, with a view to understanding the great spirit who projected them. I have attempted to point out their essential beauties and value, not from the vantage-ground of the connoisseur, but from the point of view of the sympathetic observer. I have sought to explain, to justify, the affinity felt for them by those to whom the doctrine of "Art for art's sake" is not an all-satisfying thesis, who would fain find in plastic art a language expressive of spiritual intuitions and revelation. Blake's mission undoubtedly was to discover in his representations[Pg 194] of visible phenomena the spiritual cause, or correspondence, of which it appeared to him to be merely a type. How far his ideas are consistent with the conditions and scope of an art which must necessarily concern itself with surfaces and appearances, it is hard to say. His view of art's function was largely, but not wholly true, yet in its special application was profoundly noble and salutary. Exaggerated, perhaps, in his recoil from the materialism and preoccupation with physical and natural beauties as ends in themselves which characterized the art of his day, he set to work to liberate one hitherto unsuspected aspect of art's functions, at the expense of belittling the recognized and practised articles of belief recited in her honour by the masters of his time.

The innerness of art; that is what he was concerned about. Impetuously, passionately he stormed along the rugged track he had set himself to explore, ignoring much of beauty and truth to either side of him, because his eyes were so steadfastly fixed on his goal. To-day we acclaim him as the heroic and devoted priest of a new and yet old altar to Art, the flame of which has been kept burning since his time by Dante Gabriel Rossetti and the Pre-Raphaelites, and Mr. G. F. Watts.

Made in the USA
Middletown, DE
20 August 2016